If you've ever wondered if God really c[ares]
this book is for you. Within these page[s]
live out a "holy pursuit of happiness" a[nd]
eye-opening assessment you can take to find out what happiness
style you naturally flourish in. I can't say enough good things
about *The Happiness Dare*!

LYSA TERKEURST
New York Times bestselling author and president of Proverbs 31 Ministries

Jennifer Dukes Lee's insightful and engaging words share not only
the *how* of happiness but also the *heart* of it. More than just helpful
information, *The Happiness Dare* lays out a path to spiritual and
emotional transformation. As someone for whom happiness doesn't
come naturally or easily, I wish I'd had this book years ago.

HOLLEY GERTH
Wall Street Journal bestselling author of *You're Already Amazing*

Jennifer grabbed my attention on every page with her thoughtful
and thought-provoking words on what happiness looks and feels
like. This book will inspire you to let your guard down so you'll
be empowered to experience the life-changing and God-given
happiness found throughout every season and circumstance.

MELISSA MICHAELS
New York Times bestselling author of *Love the Home You Have* and *The Inspired Room*

I was *so* blessed and challenged by reading this book. It spoke to me
at a deep level and inspired me to embark on my own Happiness
Dare! Thank you, Jennifer, for inspiring us all to boycott cynicism
and wring the delight out of the ordinary days.

CRYSTAL PAINE
New York Times bestselling author and founder of MoneySavingMom.com

In all of our striving for happiness, could it really be that God wants
us to be happy too? In *The Happiness Dare*, Jennifer Dukes Lee helps
us discover a truth a lot of us have been missing and dares us to boldly
walk in the freedom God intended for us all along. I absolutely loved
this book!

RUTH SCHWENK
Founder of TheBetterMom.com; author of *Hoodwinked* and *Pressing Pause*

In *The Happiness Dare*, Jennifer invites every kind of reader to
find happiness and the God who created it. She not only reveals

the beautifully biblical case for "happy holiness," but she invites us beyond theory and into the living.

SARA HAGERTY
Author of *Every Bitter Thing Is Sweet*

Happiness—it's that elusive destination our culture seeks at all costs. And often when we finally grasp the slippery emotion, it's fleeting. In *The Happiness Dare*, Jennifer unpacks the journey to a truly happy life found in Christ instead of our feelings. It's practical, it's encouraging, it's a dare we should all take! I highly recommend this book.

KRISTEN WELCH
Author of *Rhinestone Jesus* and *Raising Grateful Kids in an Entitled World*

The Happiness Dare is so much more than a book. Jennifer has created an insightful, fun, wise, and encouraging life-guide to help us become the best version of ourselves by living in our God-given sweet spot. Packed with powerful stories, tools, and everything you need to discover your personal happiness style, you're in for a treat. Get rid of the guilt and get ready to enjoy the way God made you!

RENEE SWOPE
Bestselling author of *A Confident Heart*

With her familiar warmth and wisdom, Jennifer Dukes Lee has written a captivating book that will transform the way you think about happiness. Combining biblical truth and brilliant storytelling, she answers all of the questions I have privately wondered about happiness, revealing how it beautifully intersects with joy and holiness in the Christian life. You don't want to miss *The Happiness Dare*. It will have you doing your own happy dance.

JEANNIE CUNNION
Author of *Parenting the Wholehearted Child*

As I read *The Happiness Dare*, I kept repeating one sentence to myself about its author: *Wow, she really gets me.* Jennifer is a most insightful and trustworthy writer, and I connected with this book in a way I've connected with few others. Not only is *The Happiness Dare* the best kind of medicine for any woman who fears happiness is unattainable or unholy; reading it is just plain *fun*. Pick up this engaging book and discover your own sweet spot of happiness: where your earthly pleasure meets heavenly joy.

KRISTEN STRONG
Author of *Girl Meets Change*

the happiness dare

Pursuing your heart's deepest, holiest,
and most vulnerable desire

JENNIFER DUKES LEE

**TYNDALE
MOMENTUM**

*An Imprint of
Tyndale House Publishers, Inc.*

Visit Tyndale online at www.tyndale.com.

Visit Tyndale Momentum online at www.tyndalemomentum.com.

Visit the author at jenniferdukeslee.com.

Tyndale Momentum and the Tyndale Momentum logo are registered trademarks of Tyndale House Publishers, Inc. Tyndale Momentum is an imprint of Tyndale House Publishers, Inc., Carol Stream, Illinois.

The Happiness Dare: Pursuing Your Heart's Deepest, Holiest, and Most Vulnerable Desire

Designed by Nicole Grimes

Published in association with the literary agency of William K. Jensen Literary Agency, 119 Bampton Court, Eugene, OR 97404.

Library of Congress Cataloging-in-Publication Data

Names: Lee, Jennifer Dukes, author.

Title: The happiness dare : pursuing your heart's deepest, holiest, and most vulnerable desire / Jennifer Dukes Lee.

Description: Carol Stream, IL : Tyndale House Publishers, Inc., 2016. | Includes bibliographical references.

Identifiers: LCCN 2016013248 | ISBN 9781496411143 (sc)

Subjects: LCSH: Christian women—Religious life. | Happiness—Religious aspects—Christianity.

Classification: LCC BV4527 .L445 2016 | DDC 248.8/43—dc23 LC record available at https://lccn.loc.gov/2016013248

Printed in the United States of America

22	21	20	19	18	17	16
7	6	5	4	3	2	1

To Mom and Dad

With God's help, I wrote this book.

With God's strength, you've lived it.

Contents

The Confession of a Happy Woman

This book scares me.

I know how crazy that probably sounds to you. This is a book about happiness, after all. Surely as you peeled open the first pages of this book, you expected to read a happy story about a happy woman who holds all the secrets to a happy life.

But instead you find me, a woman in knots.

Let me begin by setting the record straight.

Am I a happy woman? Yes. Most of the time, I am a genuinely happy woman. You are far more likely to see me with a smile than with a scowl. Science tells us that people are born with a "happiness set point." That baseline is written into our genes. Some of us start with higher set points than others. If something good happens, our happiness rises. If something awful happens, our happiness plummets. But after a while, our mood generally inches its way back to our personal genetic set point.

Genetically speaking, my happiness point is set to sunny. But I am more than a happy woman. I am a person who lives— as Ron Burgundy famously said in *Anchorman*—"in a glass case of emotion." I'm hopelessly human, which makes me terribly, wonderfully complicated.

In the last several days, a whole range of emotions has surged through me—anger, elation, despair, hilarity, guilt, and confusion. I have lost my cool with my kids, laughed so hard my belly hurt, become impatient in traffic, and experienced an all-out bawlfest during a commercial where a loving father makes origami cranes out of gum wrappers for his daughter.

I have repeatedly been described as a "passionate" woman. Which means I seriously have *all the feelings*. As I am writing these words, the emotion *du jour* is fear. That's because, of all the feelings I've ever felt, happiness is the hardest to wrap words around.

I'm scared to write a book about happiness because I know what a disaster I can be some days. Will you find me credible? Will I sound too perky—or too morose? I want to show you the messy me, the unhappy me, in the pages ahead. But will you wonder whether the sad me can lead you to a happy place? And during your own very worst day, will you get annoyed by the happy-clappy me if you meet her on a page? (If you've read my first book, *Love Idol*, you know that I've always battled my need for your approval, so I've dragged that aggravating little aspect of my personality straight into the opening pages of this book.)

Right now, I'm sitting inside a little cabin in northern Minnesota. To me, this is one of the happiest places on earth. Our family comes here at least once every summer to find peace and solace among the loons and the pine-scented air. Writing from this place, I would like to present you with a carefully constructed portrait of a pious, perfect happiness. See me, napping in a hammock after committing various Bible verses to memory. Watch me, paddle boating with the kids and winking flirtatiously at my husband. I am always with a smile, patient and tolerant of my children squabbling. In this portrait, there are no biting flies or sunburns or ruffled feelings. Of course, all of that is a misleading, incomplete picture. Can I show you more?

Last night, right here in this happy northwoods cabin, I went to bed in tears. I heard a loon crying outside my window, a haunting echo across the lake. The nearly full moon hung overhead, sprinkling diamonds of light across rippled water. I pressed my face into the pillow.

Just before bed, my husband, Scott, and I had a stupid fight. We tangled with words. It was a ridiculous argument, but it broke the irascible me open, and that spitfire passion I told you about shot out of my guts and onto the plaid comforter. I was a human volcano, the opposite of happy. I woke up this morning with yet another emotion: remorse. (And about an hour ago, I got up the nerve to apologize; therein one finds the emotion called "being humbled.")

How can this woman—mildly deranged when provoked and prone to lose her hinges—tell you what happy looks like? Can I write only on the days when my claws have retracted? Is someone perpetually sweet and affable more suited for this task? Even so, I cannot keep this to myself. You see, I took one fantastic dare. That wild dare made me feel new and warm and bright on the inside, like I swallowed a star.

So, hi, here I am—your new friend, tapping out words and embarrassingly feeling all the feelings right in front of you. A friend told me the other day that it was okay to let you know I was scared. "The last person they want to hear from is someone who has it all together." Well, then. Mission accomplished. This is me—glitchy, imperfect me.

I decided to trust my friend, and that's why this book begins with a confession. You needed to know, at the starting line, that the Happiness Dare is one thrilling ride that changed me a lot—but it still scares me a little. Because maybe? This dare will scare you a little too.

PART 1

You Have Permission

In this section of *The Happiness Dare*, we will:

Discover why happiness is such a vulnerable
and scary emotion

Learn the true relationship between
happiness and holiness

Find out how happiness relates to joy

Rediscover that God is the inventor of happiness
and that he shamelessly entices us to chase after it

Take a dare that will change our lives . . .
and our world

CHAPTER 1

Stalking Happiness

~

It was when I was happiest that I longed most. . . .
The sweetest thing in all my life has been the longing . . .
to find the place where all the beauty came from.

C. S. LEWIS

For most of my life, I considered myself a happy person—not the kind of woman who claps with giddy delight over her breakfast waffles, but the kind of woman who makes regular use of her grin.

I grew up in a happy home with two parents who loved me. My life wasn't perfect, but I was exceedingly blessed. Mom and Dad took us every Sunday morning to the brick-front Methodist church, which sat a block away from our home. Sunday afternoons were spent with the radio tuned to 94.5 FM for Casey Kasem's *American Top 40*.

There were countless games of tag and Ghost in the Graveyard. My hair was held firmly in place by Aqua Net, and I kept my limbs cozy inside of leg warmers. The town library was three blocks from my front door, and we were permitted to climb onto the roof of our house to read our books. I slid every morning down a wooden banister. My mom was the town prankster—every summer she planted a plastic tomato in the neighbors' garden, giving them the false hope of the town's first crop. Dad drove a silver Mercury and taught us about hard work and loyalty. He worked for the same farmers' co-op for all of my growing-up years. A banana-seat bike carted me a good many miles around my hometown. My cat answered to Garfield.

We didn't have air-conditioning, but that meant I fell asleep on May nights with windows cracked open wide enough for the rain and lilacs to sneak in on a fragrant ribbon, floating under my nose during dreams.

But there were hard days too—a tapestry of funerals, break-ups, surgeries, and teenage counseling appointments for my anxiety. I still have the cassette tapes my therapist used to try and hypnotize me into a better frame of mind. But even then, I had it in me solid to believe that life was generally good, and that it was all going to work out in the end.

As an adult, I've seen life mostly through the same rose-colored lenses. To me, the proverbial glass has usually been half-full. Sure, there have been hard seasons. I could spend whole chapters telling you about the mess of my marriage in the early years, Scott's and my dual workaholism, and a long stretch of postpartum depression after our daughter Anna was born. I took a little yellow pill to keep me level. But even during those inevitable times when the glass looked half-empty, I was always thankful that I had a glass—and that there was something in it.

Then I entered middle adulthood. I held the same glass as before, but it felt like the contents were leaking through a hole I couldn't find. I had fallen into a bland malaise—me, a chronic

Eeyore—but not for any one particular reason. I wasn't exactly despairing, but I knew I wasn't as happy as I could be. I wondered if maybe this was what people called a midlife crisis. I wasn't sure.

There were legitimate reasons for my sludgy feelings. I had entered a season of protracted loneliness. My husband's dad, Paul, became sick with leukemia and then died within the year, leaving a hole in our hearts. My husband scrambled to figure out how to farm seven hundred acres of land on his own. Four days before Paul died, a car flew into my lane on an icy highway, crashing into my van. I was grateful to have survived, but I ended up with a wound that took six months to heal. The whole ordeal caused me to consider how fragile life was—and how quickly mine was passing by. I began to rethink my life's purpose, my plans, and whether I was living the life God wanted for me.

You know how it goes: In one skinny minute, a crisis can grow out of nowhere to devour your happiness. All over the planet, right this instant, happiness is being snatched away by a tumor with long fingers, by a spouse with stubborn addictions, or by a coworker with a mean streak who makes the office feel like a hike through the Mojave Desert—while wearing stilettos.

But sometimes it's the little irritations that chisel away at your joy: Your jeans don't fit like they used to. You miss your flight. You lose your cool. You burn the pizza. You sell out. You think un-Christian thoughts in church. One kid kicks the other in the shins, and your own personal meltdown makes theirs look like an English tea party. Your favorite show is canceled. Someone you care about doesn't invite you. You shrink your favorite T-shirt. You envy how everyone else seems to be finding the secret to a happy life—and how it comes so naturally to them, with perfectly plated suppers and exotic beach vacations. You experience guilt when you live the opposite of what you preach to your kids—hypothetically speaking, of course. All of it makes you feel shadowy on the inside, not exactly like the person you want to be.

During my own gloomy season, questions clinked around in my insides, like ice against glass, about the meaning of life. Was Solomon—the king with enough status and wealth to seek happiness in every earthly pleasure imaginable—right? Was it all "Meaningless! Meaningless!"?[1]

As I asked these questions, I was certain that my life wasn't bearing the fruit of happiness like it could. And I wondered if part of the problem was my misinterpretation of what it meant to live happily in Jesus. I knew what the Bible said about picking up my cross and walking the narrow way home. When Jesus came again, I was pretty sure he'd rather find me suffering for him than swinging merrily from the rafters. Yet in my wearying efforts at lugging around my piety, I felt like I was missing something crucial.

My life was—statistically speaking—half over, and I was afraid I had been sleepwalking through it. My productivity would tell you otherwise. My productivity would tell you I was a *machine*. I was operating as if my worth—and my happiness—could be calculated in efficiencies, proficiencies, boxes checked, and ladders climbed. Ask me to serve on your committee, and I would shout, "Yes!" You needed someone to take the lead? You could count on me! Who needed sleep? I could sleep when I was dead.

Night after night, I awoke to see the clock staring back at me: 2:28 a.m.

3:19 a.m.

4:25 a.m.

During those hours, I would roll over to stare across the darkened room. The trees, illuminated by the outdoor lamplight, cast lacy shadows that shuffled across the wall next to the metal cross. My mind replayed events of the day previous. When I was done with yesterday's missteps and mistakes, I would fixate on the worst-case scenarios of tomorrow.

I'd quickly remind myself that life was too short to fret like this. I even knew the Bible verses that said so. I'll bet you have them underlined too. "Do not worry about tomorrow." "My yoke is easy and my burden is light."[2] Those were the kinds of verses I shared with people nearly every day on my blog and social-media pages. Before I ever write a message quoting Scripture to my readers, you can be fairly certain that I have preached the same words to the most bankrupt parts of myself. A lot of that preaching happened in the dark hours at the Church of St. Mattress.

I didn't want my tombstone to read, "Here lies a woman who had great intentions but lived with deep regret." Also? I wanted to have more fun before I was in said grave, taking—as my mother would say—my "dirt nap." I wanted to be a woman who lived joyfully until I drew my last breath.

My self-affirming pep talks generally lulled me back to sleep, with my peace temporarily intact and my resolve strengthened. But by morning, my inner crazy was coming in through the back door of my brain. Before 9:00 a.m., I found myself barking orders at the girls, bemoaning my deadlines, and deepening the crease on my forehead. My disordered thoughts robbed me of the ability to enjoy life, despite the innumerable blessings I'd been given: a good man, two beautiful girls, health, a roof over my head, and a church family. Yet I was missing my life. I was missing God.

At night, I'd fall back asleep, trees waving outside in the breeze, only to wake up again with those alarm-clock numbers staring back at me as I quoted verses, made promises, and vowed again that tomorrow would be different.

I had lost the fullness of my happiness and I didn't know where to find it. What I'm going to tell you next might sound a little crazy, but it's the truth: During those times of unhappiness, my great comfort came in believing that God didn't care about happiness anyway. My great comfort came in believing that God cared more about my holiness. So I figured, *If I can't be happy, I'm still good with God.* My holiness, then, became an excuse to stop seeking happiness.

This is a tragic error of Christians everywhere. Welcome to the atrophy of the human soul. But this is where some of us are right now. We are highly suspicious of happiness. We really *do* want to be happy—secretly of course—but we'll tell everyone else it's joy we want. Because isn't joy the holier aim? Isn't happiness against the rules?

Some of us may believe that we have to pick one or the other: happiness or Jesus. During my gray days, I didn't know yet that there was a third option: happy holiness. When I discovered happy holiness, it felt like fireworks were going off inside my chest. I had come to understand this truth: Our inner desire for happiness isn't a sin. It's a desire planted in us by God himself.

Yes, you read that right: happiness. Not the reverse of joy. Not the opposite of holiness. But authentic happiness, found in Jesus.

What We're All After

We've just met, but there's something I know about you. You want to be happy too.

How can I be so sure of that? Over thousands of years, people have craved it, sung about it, prayed for it, and wished upon the shimmering stars for it: happiness. It's the underline of every New Year's resolution, the reason behind every diet, the hope underneath every "I do" at the altar. Happiness is the aim of every human—from the free-wheeling squanderer to the most saintly woman under your church steeple.

You and I just want to be happy.

I don't know one person in my life who prefers an unhappy marriage to a happy one; an unhappy heart to a happy one; an unhappy workplace; or unhappy kids. I don't know a sane soul who would dare say, "I wish I wasn't so happy."

Blaise Pascal wrote it more bluntly:

All men seek happiness. This is without exception.
Whatever different means they employ, they all tend
to this end. The cause of some going to war, and of
others avoiding it, is the same desire in both, attended
with different views. The will never takes the least step
but to this object. This is the motive of every action of
every man, even of those who hang themselves.[3]

Yikes to the hanging part. But still. It's this longing for happiness that drives us. It's the core motivation behind the colleges we pick, the career paths we choose, the clubs we join, the friends we associate with, the people we marry, even the sacrifices we make for others. We might call it purpose, contentment, peace, joy—but if Pascal and dozens of other philosophers are right, we are motivated by what we think will create more happiness for ourselves and for those we love.

But this happiness we seek is not a wimpy emotion. Happiness has been advertised as some kittenish, fluffy feeling. In reality, happiness can make your heart race with excitement—and sometimes with a bit of fear. Because on our happiest days, we are worried it won't last. My husband and I will go long stretches of argue-free days—and not just argue-free days, but truly happy and blissful days, days when I thank the good Lord for giving me the man I have. He's so precious to me. But on those days, I'm also scared to live into the fullness of my happiness. I hold back my enthusiasm, an emotional tempering, because I'm afraid of what's ahead.

Quarrels like the one we had in the northwoods remind me that the future is always ticking toward the inevitable argument and the forgiveness that will surely need to be asked for. Even worse, we know happiness can be fleeting because trouble awaits us all.

"In this world you will have trouble,"[4] Jesus said.

Not "might."

Not "if you're especially naughty."

Not "probably."

Jesus said you *will* have trouble. As a result, happiness leaves us vulnerable.

Why Happiness Is a Vulnerable Desire

Happiness is a vulnerable desire because crisis is an absolute guarantee.

We all know we might be one phone call, one diagnosis, or one fight away from losing what feels so good right now. How can I live with extravagant happiness today if the remote possibility exists that one of my two girls has a yet-undetected terminal illness? I can't tell you how many times I've gotten up at 3:00 a.m., playing out worst-case scenarios that are not likely to ever unfold.

But the truth is, my worst nightmares are someone's present reality. What right do I have to be happy in a busted-up world where people are weeping over graves right this second?

If we are in a season of great blessing, we might feel guilty for it when we look around at a warped world filled with pain. Dare I be happy when people are starving, dying, or running for their lives from terrorists?

Furthermore, if God wants us to be happy, what does that say about us when we are unhappy? If we are not happy today, does that mean that we are doing something wrong? If God wants us to be happy and we are just not "feeling it" for a day, or for a whole season, does that mean we've been found disobedient to an all-seeing God?

If God wants people to be happy, but we're miserable, it is easy to believe that one of these two hypotheses is true:

1. I'm doing life all wrong.

or

2. God doesn't really see me or love me. He sees and loves all the other happy people, with their unfiltered profile pics; trophied kids; second honeymoons; job

promotions; and perfectly plated, Instagrammable dinners. But if my own life is a mess, maybe God doesn't see or love me.

There are two more reasons why happiness is such a vulnerable desire:

1. **In moments where we dare to feel happy, someone else might resent us for it.** If you've ever been the target of someone's envy, you know what I mean. You got the promotion, reached a new fitness goal, or received special recognition. You were happy, for good reason. But not everyone shared in your happiness. You could practically feel their envy from across the room. If that's you, these words, attributed to actress Bette Midler, will make a ton of sense: "The worst part of success is trying to find someone who is happy for you."

    Furthermore, we may feel bad when we know that the source of our happiness is the prayed-for dream of someone we know. I remember, for instance, feeling a tempered happiness when I found out that I was pregnant after Scott and I had tried for exactly a month. When I saw the faint lines show up on my pregnancy test, I rejoiced. But then I started counting. Immediately I could name five women who had been trying to have a baby for months, even years.

    Happiness makes us feel vulnerable because we don't know how to appropriately express ourselves when someone else can't have what we have. We don't want our happiness to be the source of someone else's unhappiness.

2. **Happiness leaves us feeling vulnerable because it actually does have a shadow side.** There's a negative form of happiness, a "do whatever makes you happy" philosophy that really *is* selfish. We all know people who have looked for happiness in ill-advised places.

In the enemy's hands, what God meant for good is always used for evil. It's one of the enemy's favorite tricks—to make you misuse a gift from your Creator. The main problem with happiness isn't in our *desire*. It's in the ways we sometimes try to feed that desire.

At the root of idolatry is the cunning twisting of truth. Cool gifts from God—like sex, food, and even happiness—become nooses slipped around our spiritual necks. The enemy convinces us that anything God made is better in excess.

What we think will bring us happiness is sometimes short-lived, if not dangerous. (I can say that, because I once tried to ride a mechanical bull. My happiness lasted approximately 3.5 seconds, followed by an intense case of unhappiness in my right hip. But I digress.)

We can see how the chase for happiness has moved people miles away from God. We look around and see the carnage left behind when people indulge the carnal pursuit of happiness: the broken families, empty bottles, and drained checkbooks.

But wait. That doesn't mean we ought to turn our backs on the worthy pursuit of happiness. Author Randy Alcorn writes, "Is there selfish and superficial happiness? Sure. There's also selfish and superficial love, peace, loyalty, and trust. We shouldn't throw out

Christ-centered happiness with the bathwater of self-centered happiness."[5]

Humans are great mistreaters and mistrusters of the virtue of happiness. When life is good, we feel guilty about being happy. When life is bad, someone else will remind us that another person has it worse. And if we stay unhappy too long, we can feel forced by someone to *get happy, for heaven's sake!*

Dear humans everywhere: The pursuit of happiness is not for wimps.

Happiness Is . . .

Charles Schulz said that happiness is a warm puppy. I think that it's more like a roaring lion.

Happiness is terrifying, like coming face-to-face with something that can eat you for breakfast. But dare we climb up on the back of the lion? When we're riding on the back of that lion, we're giving in to a fiercely courageous emotion called happiness.

What is happiness?

Happiness is the feeling of contentment that wells up inside of you when you are at peace with who you are and the life you've been given.

Happiness is a feeling, but it's also a decision. It's a choice we get to make every day, even on our hardest days.

Happiness is an outward expression of an inward joy that is found in Jesus.

Happiness is a gift from a happy God.

Happiness is an offer extended to us by the gospel—an offer of happiness forever, starting with happiness today. God has been daring me to find it, to grab hold of the golden mane of Aslan[6] and ride the hills. Can I show you more? In the pages ahead, I will invite you to take an actual dare. It's called the Happiness Dare—a journey that will take you toward your heart's deepest desire.

We'll unpack this dare in more detail in chapter 3, but let me give you a sneak preview: The source of your happiness is already inside you—and it won't demand that you try harder or pretend you're someone else.

This is not a dare to find self-centered happiness. Every year, I meet thousands of people while I serve as a speaker at conferences and retreats across North America. Many of these people share their hearts with me, and at root, all of them desire happiness. But these people are not self-centered. They are not on some vain hunt for flimsy, buy-it-at-the-store happiness.

These people are *you and me.*

They are doing a lot of the right things but feeling as if it's all falling apart. They are faithful in prayer and diligent in serving while caring for kids, aging parents, or both. They are trying to hold down jobs while also ensuring that the dishes are washed and the lawn is mowed. Many of the people I meet are women who see themselves as the keepers of everyone else's happiness, so they are knocking themselves out with a lot of overhustle.

These people struggle with crazy schedules, suffering marriages, prodigal children, weight gain, and financial loss. They are *just like you*—overworked, overwhelmed, overcommitted, and overextended. They thirst for happiness, but they don't know if God even wants to satisfy that thirst—because it feels selfish to ask.

But what if we didn't merely ask for happiness? What if we stalked it? Early on during this Happiness Dare, I happened upon a letter written by Flannery O'Connor. Her words made my heart bounce around inside of me: "Picture me with my ground teeth stalking joy—fully armed, too, as it's a highly dangerous quest."[7]

Flannery was grinding her teeth with a singular purpose: the stalking of joy.

I have hopped on the back of a lion to stalk joy and *happiness*, even if it's a dangerous quest.

Road Map to Happiness

There are treasures for you in this book, oh, lion rider. I invite you to ride a glorious path strewn with gladness and delight. Knowing where we're headed will be helpful for both of us, so I've made a map centered on the three parts of this book.

Part 1: You Have Permission. This is where we are now. We are just beginning to rethink happiness, and we're about to be reintroduced to the one who invented happiness. God doesn't just approve of our happiness. He shamelessly entices us to chase after it. For some of us, this is a game-changing perspective shifter. So many of us are missing the pleasure of a life in Christ because we have long thought that happiness is mostly a self-centered, carnal pursuit.

Many people, including me, need permission to be happy. We need to know that we are not at odds with the gospel if we seek authentic happiness. Happiness isn't unholy. It's gravely misunderstood. We're spending these first chapters rethinking happiness and reclaiming our God-given right to experience it. Part 1 of this book is the permission we all need to take the Happiness Dare.

Part 2: You Have a Style. This is where things get exciting for us as we begin to live happier lives. We will learn that we each have our own happiness styles. We are all wired by God for happiness, but what brings us happiness varies widely.

Our "What's Your Happiness Style?" assessment will pinpoint how you are wired. You'll learn what your own personal happiness style reveals about you. The easiest way to take the assessment is to visit us online at www.thehappinessdare.com. This survey will pinpoint your happiness style within five minutes. (The assessment is also found in the back of this book.) Knowing your style will help you live more fully into the life God has given you, even on your hardest days.

Part 3: You Have a Choice. Here we'll explore how to apply our happiness practically in our everyday lives. We will look at four of the major obstacles standing in the way of our happiness. And together, we will move past those obstacles to live a fuller, richer version of happiness that changes our lives—and our world.

What's at Stake

Our happiness has great power. Happiness can change this tired world, a world that has become overrun with cynicism and heartache. How can happiness change the world, you ask? A girl named Anne Frank spelled it out in eight words: "Whoever is happy will make others happy too."[8]

Dare takers are world changers. No matter how happy or unhappy we are in this moment, our multiplied happiness matters more than we can imagine. Our world needs a huge happiness upgrade. Amen? Everywhere we look, we see people malnourished in happiness—sometimes in our own bathroom mirrors. We've lost the buoyancy of spirit that Charles Spurgeon spoke of in the nineteenth century: "Those who are 'beloved of the Lord' must be the most happy and joyful people to be found anywhere upon the face of the earth!" If ever we needed happy people down here, it is now.

Happiness breeds happiness. But you know what else? Unhappiness breeds unhappiness. Whatever we feel inside of us ripples outside of us.

Happiness is not a weak "feeling." It's revolutionary. No matter how happy or unhappy you are today, you will benefit from a boost in your happiness. Your happiness matters because it changes you, it transforms our world, and it glorifies our Maker.

Together, we can begin to "circumstance-proof" our happiness. We can refuse to link our happiness with the events and incidents in our lives. Instead, we can build a more valuable virtue within ourselves—a virtue that is like Teflon to all the biting cynicism of the world.

This Happiness Dare takes courage. It takes courage to wake up and say, "Happiness isn't in things. Happiness isn't in circumstances. Happiness isn't in money or status or popularity. Happiness is in me."

Happiness might be the bravest decision you'll ever make.

Digging Deeper •••••••••••••••••

1. Jennifer says that for most of her life she had considered
    herself a happy person, but she had lost some of that
    happiness along the way. Take a self-inventory of your
    happiness. How happy have you been in the key seasons
    of your life, and how happy are you today?

2. Do you think God cares about your happiness, your
    holiness, or both? Do you feel like you must pick between
    happiness and Jesus?

3. Jennifer describes happiness as a vulnerable desire.
    Have you experienced the vulnerable side of happiness?
    If so, when?

4. Think of the happiest people in your life. How has their
    happiness been contagious?

CHAPTER 2

The Holy Pursuit of Happiness

᳙

The single most important principle I ever discovered is this: the goal or purpose of the Christian is precisely the pursuit of happiness—in God. The reason for this is that there is no greater way to glorify God than to find in Him the happiness that my soul so desperately craves.

SAM STORMS

If you want to figure out what happiness looks like, go to a wedding. The candles, the vows, flower girls tossing petals, little boys wearing tuxedos, the bride and groom believing that happily ever after is possible. I can't think of a better place to witness happiness this side of heaven.

Last summer, I attended the wedding of a friend's daughter. As we waited for the bride to walk down the aisle, the sanctuary was a hum of excited whispers. I glanced to my right, and the stained-glass windows caught my eye.

The late-afternoon sunlight slanted in perfectly, giving the colorful scenes a glowing aura. As the first notes of *Canon in D* filled the sanctuary, my eyes skipped from window to window. What I saw startled me. In every scene, Jesus wore a melancholy or stern expression. The stained-glass Jesus looked like he regretted his decision to visit earth.

In one image, Jesus' knuckles rapped against a wooden door. He wore the countenance of a door-to-door vacuum salesman—worn out from a long day of work—rather than of someone who loved the people on the inside of the house.

Meanwhile, here we were, the people of Jesus, in the house of Jesus, gathered in his name and for his glory and the union of two pretty cool people. Most of us wore a very different kind of expression from the stained-glass Jesuses. Our faces revealed delight and pleasure.

It occurred to me, in those moments before the bride entered the sanctuary, that our skewed views on happiness might somehow be linked to a misinformed idea about the way God looks at us.

Take a moment to think about your answers to the following questions: Do you envision God as a happy Father? Did Jesus roam from place to place, looking for the next table to overturn? Does the Holy Spirit only convict, or does he also delight? Do you view yourself only as a "sinner in the hands of an angry God," or have you fully realized that you are a sinner-made-saint in the arms of a loving God? If you are to imitate Christ, what kind of Christ will you imitate? A miserable one or a happy one?

These are the kinds of questions we all need to ask before we take the Happiness Dare. Because if God doesn't give two hoots about our happiness, this dare and this book are pointless.

All of these questions ran through my mind as the wedding I've described began. Just then, we rose to our feet as the bride began her walk down the aisle, escorted by her dad. Her hair flowed down her back in long ringlets. Candles flickered under the ceiling fans. After the bride and her father reached the front of the church, the pastor asked us to bow our heads in prayer. But instead of praying to a stern Jesus, the pastor prayed to a joyful one: "Just as you gladdened the wedding at Cana in Galilee . . . bring your joy to this wedding."

The words got jammed in my heart. Jesus had *what*? What was that he did? The pastor had said it: Jesus "gladdened the wedding." Gladdened! He didn't come to critique the food, or shame the decorator, or tell someone she forgot to wear her Spanx. He wasn't standing guard at the door like a bouncer. He didn't wet-blanket the wedding. He *gladdened* it!

That Saturday, in the filtered late-afternoon light of the sanctuary, I began to wonder if we've made Jesus out to be a happiness hater.

Our Master's Happiness

Religion can be an overridingly serious business. Now, I am serious about my Jesus. But so many of us have grown up on a steady diet of "thou shalt nots," in which our religious teachers showed us what was off-limits rather than showing us how we might flourish in God's abundance. Some of us grew up believing that we were meant for martyrdom more than merriment.

We've sat under teachings that created a dichotomy between holiness and happiness. Happiness seemed off-limits, even sinful.

Sitting under the steeple during that wedding, I quietly pulled the Bible from the wooden book holder attached to the pew in front of me. Flipping through the pages, words like *happy, glad, feasting, pleasure, joy,* and *delight* flashed in front of my eyes. And even when the words weren't used explicitly, I knew inherently that nearly every page of Scripture revealed the reason for a human being's deepest happiness. On the pages of our Bibles, we see a faithful God, a sovereign God, a loving God, a delighting God, a listening God, a saving God, a redeeming God, a God who is "for us," . . . even a happy God.

I turned to the Gospel of Matthew, and the words leaped from the page. "Come and share your master's happiness!"[1]

I flipped back to a familiar verse in Zephaniah: "The LORD your God is with you, the Mighty Warrior who saves. He will take great delight in you; in his love he will no longer rebuke you, but will rejoice over you with singing."[2]

What kind of God delights over his people with singing? What kind of God declares his people, at the beginning of creation, as not only good but "very good"? What kind of God is portrayed over and over again in the Scriptures?

Our happy God. That's who.

"May the righteous be glad and rejoice before God; may they be happy and joyful" (Psalm 68:3).

"Be glad; rejoice forever in my creation! And look! I will create Jerusalem as a place of happiness. Her people will be a source of joy" (Isaiah 65:18, NLT).

God lifted the blindfold during that wedding. I began to see his personality come into clearer focus. Ours is a glad God, not a grumpy one.

That night at the wedding dance, we feasted on roast beef. We savored the frosting on the cake. We danced the Electric Slide and flapped our arms to the Chicken Dance. A group of us cried happy tears when the father of the bride asked his daughter for a dance. We were set below the twinkling lights, amid the song, among the happy people of God, for the glory of our happy God.

Together, we shared in the master's happiness.

The Happiness of Jesus

We've been taught how to suffer like Jesus, for the glory of Jesus. To be sure, the Scriptures reveal a suffering Jesus. But the Scriptures also reveal a happy Jesus.

Jesus' first miracle wasn't at a grave site. It was at a party. Remember the wedding that he gladdened? Here's what happened.

Back in Jesus' day, weddings were a big deal. They started at sundown with a ceremony at the synagogue. Then the couple would parade through the city, along with the wedding guests. Afterward, the party began. And it wasn't a four-hour shindig with bell-shaped mints, a punch bowl, a deejay, and a disco ball. The party lasted for days. People would deliver speeches, eat rich foods, and drink wine. Hosts took their roles seriously. It was considered bad manners to exhaust the supply of food or wine.

But something embarrassing happened at the wedding in Cana. The hosts ran out of wine. And Mary, the mother of Jesus, found out about the faux pas. So she marched over to her son to tell him what happened: "They have no more wine" (John 2:3).

At first Jesus said it was not his time to perform miracles. But then, for some reason, he reconsidered. He ordered some helpers to get jars filled with water. He then turned the water to wine—and not just any wine, but the best wine.

Jesus gladdened a wedding. Jesus was the life of the party, and if you belong to Jesus, the life of the party lives in you.

Jesus was the kind of guy who didn't despise parties or jubilant crowds or noisy children. He was regularly in the company of friends. He enjoyed the dinner table and the breaking of bread. Imagine the happiness at the occasion of a child's healing, at the side of Lazarus's tomb, at the home of the Emmaus travelers. See Jesus, surrounded by children, when he said, "Let the little children come to me."[3] What child would ever draw near to a killjoy Jesus?

Examining the Scriptures in light of my Happiness Dare, this is what I began to find:

Happiness isn't unholy. It's just misunderstood.

What if we began to imagine Jesus with us when we are enjoying what we enjoy? What if, starting today, you tried placing a chair (or picturing one) in whatever room you're in and inviting Jesus into the chair? Imagine him sitting with you. Imagine Jesus with you, wherever you are, not as a watchdog for your behavior, but as a friend, delighting in what brings you delight.

Share in your master's happiness, and let him share in yours.

Thy Happy Kingdom Come

Days after my realization at the wedding, I dug deeper into Scripture and found that Jesus' teachings suggest his own happiness. Some of his stories are downright amusing and would have been considered hilarious to a first-century audience.[4] Some scholars say that Jesus' illustrations were intentionally ridiculous. A camel going through the eye of a needle? Lighting a lamp under a basket? A father who gives a child stones instead of bread? These scholars say Jesus' audience would have laughed at the artful use of humor and wit.

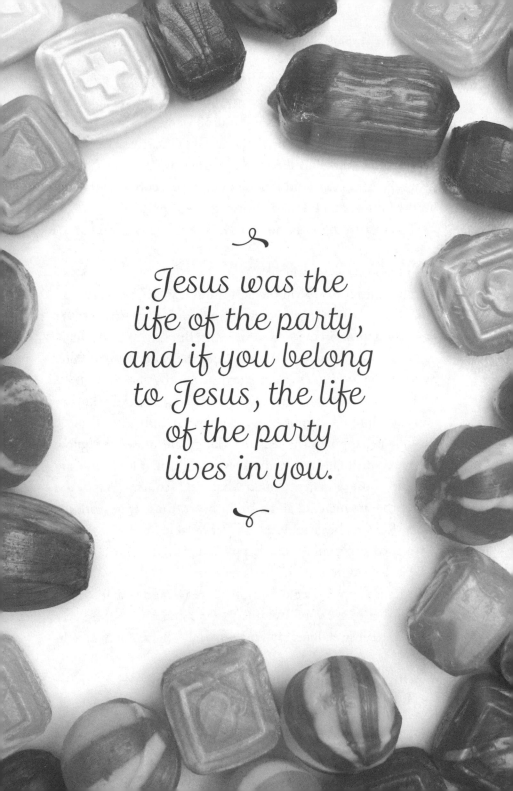

Jesus was the
life of the party,
and if you belong
to Jesus, the life
of the party
lives in you.

Indeed, Scripture reveals that Jesus was not only holy, but happy. Never do the Scriptures pit holiness against happiness. Yes, Jesus was a man of sorrows, but he was also a man of joy.

Jesus' most famous sermon happened in the region of Galilee on a mount. Envision the crowds gathering to hear what the Nazarene has to say. Find a patch of grass or a comfortable rock on the hillside and listen as Jesus begins to speak.

The first word out of his mouth is not *holy*. It is not *joyful*. It is *happy*.

"Happy are those who . . ."[5]

The word for *happy* in the Scriptures is the Greek *makarios*. Some translations use the English word *blessed* whenever *makarios* appears in the New Testament. But other translators— keenly aware that *makarios* comes from the word *makar* (which means *happy* or *blessed*)—translate the word to *happiness* instead.

It's on that mount where Jesus opens a profoundly important door into the happiness we can have in him.

This is happiness, he tells us: Happy are those who know they are spiritually poor, those who mourn, those who are humble, those who desire to do what God requires. Happy are those who are merciful and pure in heart, those who work for peace. Remarkably, happiness is also available for those who are persecuted and insulted. "Be happy and glad, for a great reward is kept for you in heaven," Jesus tells us.[6]

Is Jesus happy? Theologian John Piper would take it a mile-step further to ask you, "Who is the happiest human who ever lived?" The answer, Piper says unequivocally, is Jesus of Nazareth.

Jesus Christ is the happiest being in the universe.

His gladness is greater than all the angelic gladness

of heaven. He mirrors perfectly the infinite, holy, indomitable mirth of his Father.[7]

Piper also says that Jesus "is, and always will be, indestructibly happy."[8]

That view is not unique to Piper. It has been a resoundingly popular view of scholars of centuries past. These scholars understood Scripture to reveal a Jesus who cared about both our holiness and our happiness. They understood that Jesus did not separate one from the other.

Biblical scholar Matthew Henry said it like this centuries ago: "Those only are happy, truly happy, that are holy, truly holy."[9]

Soon after I took the Happiness Dare, I learned of a lengthy Christian defense for happiness in a book by that name. In *Happiness*, Randy Alcorn writes:

For too long we've distanced the gospel from what Augustine, Aquinas, Pascal, the Puritans, Wesley, Spurgeon, and many other spiritual giants said God created us to desire—and what he desires for us—happiness.

To declare joy sacred and happiness secular closes the door to dialogue with unbelievers. If someone is told that joy is the opposite of happiness, any thoughtful person would say, "In that case, I don't want joy!"

If we say the gospel won't bring happiness, any perceptive listener should respond, "Then how is it good news?"

We need to reverse the trend. Let's redeem the word *happiness* in light of both Scripture and church history. Our message shouldn't be "Don't seek happiness," but "You'll find in Jesus the happiness you've always longed for."[10]

So much that Jesus taught us—in his commands, parables, and hillside lessons—was aimed directly at this target: joy and happiness. We know it for sure because of what Jesus told the disciples around the table the night he was betrayed: "I have told you this so that my joy may be in you and that your joy may be complete."[11]

I know what you're probably thinking there: *But Jesus said, "that your joy may be complete," not your happiness.* Believe me, I understand that it's problematic for some of us to equate joy and happiness. We've been trained to resist the word *happiness* in a sacred context.

I told a woman at the gym the other day that I was writing about happiness, and she asked the question that maybe you are asking: "Oh, so you actually mean joy, right?"

No, I mean happiness. While most Christians would encourage us to "choose joy," they might give us the side eye if we admit out loud that we also want happiness. Maybe you are one of those side-eyers. I used to be a skeptic too.

A few months ago, after I had begun to write the first chapters of this book, I was browsing through my boards on Pinterest, where I keep collections of favorite quotes and Bible verses. I came across a graphic, which I had posted several years earlier, with these words: "God doesn't call us to be happy. He calls us to be holy."

When I saw the graphic, I laughed out loud at the computer screen. Me, the author of a book on happiness, had once promoted a message entirely opposite to the one I was about to write! Hello. I promptly deleted the pin from my Pinterest board because God had flipped the happiness script in my mind.

Because here is the truth that no one told us (or at least that no one told me):

Happiness isn't the opposite of holy. It's a part of what makes you holy.

Happiness isn't the opposite of joy. It's a part of Christ-inspired joy, expressed within you.

Happiness isn't selfish or stupid or wrong or ridiculous.

When we seek it, we are more, not less, like Jesus.

Our happiness is hemmed directly into the heart of joy. How many truly joyful people do you know who are pinch-faced Christians? If you have to dig a mile deep to find a person's smile, is that really joy? Or has misery disguised itself as "deep Christian joy"?

I read and reread these words from Joni Eareckson Tada the other day:

We're often taught to be careful of the difference between joy and happiness. Happiness, it is said, is an emotion that depends upon what "happens." Joy, by contrast, is supposed to be enduring, stemming from deep within our soul and not affected by the circumstances surrounding us. . . . I don't think God had any such hairsplitting in mind. Scripture uses the terms interchangeably, along with words like delight, gladness, blessed. There is no scale of relative spiritual

values applied to any of these. Happiness is not
relegated to flesh-minded sinners nor joy to heaven-
bound saints.[12]

Happiness is not the great opposite of holiness. Happiness is at the heart of Jesus, who gladdens weddings. Does he not also gladden lives today? Does he not also gladden cookouts and flash mobs and moments of significant scientific discovery? Does he not also gladden birthing rooms and seaside retreats and majestic cathedrals where composers performed some of the greatest musical works of our time?

Will he not also gladden us? I believe he will.

Jesus doesn't gladden us at the expense of holiness. He gladdens us *because of* holiness. Piper says it like this: "Happiness is part of holiness . . . if you tried to describe what it means to be a holy person and left out happiness in God, you can't do it. There is no such thing as holiness minus happiness in God. Happiness in God is the essence of holiness."[13]

All of this, it could be positively life changing. This discovery of a happy Jesus caused me to read Scripture in a whole new way—and to examine my own life through the prism of Christ's happiness.

Remember the hillside sermon from Jesus? After he defined happiness, Jesus taught us to pray. "Your kingdom come . . . on earth as it is in heaven,"[14] Jesus said.

What is the Kingdom of Heaven, if not a happy place? What is heaven, if not a place of bliss where every tear is wiped away?

I tried for a moment today to imagine a God who would desire his people to be both holy and miserable. That seemed sadistic. Sure, God knew we would face misery on earth. But does he desire our misery? It seems unconscionable. In this world, we live under the curse of evil, but God does not delight in our unhappiness.

Our happy God desires happy children.

You are the *imago dei*. You carry the DNA of your happy and holy God. Do not imagine the Lord as some miserly mall security cop, with his arms crossed over his chest and a whistle around his neck, waiting for you to mess things up down here. God is the inventor of happiness and the chief spreader of it. When you desire happiness, you are not a pleasure-seeking heretic. You are responding to something built into your soul. Your desire to live happy is not a flaw. It is your soul's memory of the original paradise, etched and alive in you.

Your desire for happiness is also a hint at what's to come— the full joy you will have one day in your forever home. For a moment, try to imagine an unhappy heaven. Try hard to find the dour faces, funeral dirges, gray days, empty tables, and the lonely curmudgeons walking along littered streets. Picture St. Peter at the pearly gates with a scowl. Try to imagine Jesus angrily hanging a Do Not Disturb sign on his front door. Any luck believing in that version of heaven? I didn't think so.

Thus I pray, "Your *happy* kingdom come, on earth as it is in heaven."

To be sure, our unhappiness and our frowns will be confiscated at the gates of heaven. Why don't we get a head start on our happiness inheritance now?

Yes, God commands us to pick up our crosses and walk the narrow way home. And of course every trial we face on earth first passed through his fingers; some of the best lessons we learn in life will come in the hardest, unhappiest places on earth.

Many of us will say that we felt God's presence most profoundly in the middle of our greatest trials.

But we don't find God only in the hard. We find him also in the happy.

This discovery of our happy Jesus caused me to read Scripture in a whole new way and to examine my own life through the prism of Christ's happiness.

This discovery made me feel alive and warm—a bit glittery on the inside. Eventually it led me to make—and take—the Happiness Dare.

Digging Deeper • • • • • • • • • • • • • • • • • • •

1. What adjectives would you use to describe God? How does it feel to describe him as "happy"?

2. Why might some people have a hard time describing God as a happy Father, or Jesus as a happy man?

3. Jennifer says that our happiness is hemmed directly into the heart of joy. She asserts that happiness isn't the opposite of joy, but a part of joy. How would you compare happiness to joy?

CHAPTER 3

The Happiness Dare

⤳

It is a Christian duty, as you know, for everyone to be as happy as he can.
C. S. LEWIS

This is it. This is the chapter where I extend the dare to you.

This dare was years in the making and was taken on a whim, on a random morning when I tossed out a prayer I had never before thought to pray.

God, do you want me to be happy?

That was the question on my lips.

I stood barefoot in my pajamas at the kitchen window, looking out over our farm fields in northwest Iowa, after another fretful night of tossing about. My shadow fell across the rustic maple planks of the floor. The dark sky was brightening into the full flame of morning.

Like I did most mornings, I poured out my heart to God. I

prayed the sort of simple prayers common to us all—for good health, for safe travels, for marriages, for help and protection, for our children to stay close to Jesus. I am earnest in prayer, and though my faith is sometimes as small as a mustard seed, I try to trust Jesus at his word when he says, "Ask and it will be given to you."[1]

But that day I realized there was something I desperately wanted but had never bothered to ask Jesus for directly: happiness.

Maybe I had never asked because I didn't think I deserved happiness. Maybe I'd heard too many sermons telling me that I'd be far better off aiming for the more durable virtue of joy. If I prayed for happiness, I feared I might sound like a woman who believed in a prosperity gospel, which promises happiness through money and success. But I didn't believe that kind of gospel at all. I didn't want happiness at the expense of holiness. I wanted happiness as a part of being a human created to "glorify God and enjoy Him forever."[2]

That morning, for the first time in my life, I asked God explicitly for happiness. I told God my deepest desire: "I want to be happy." And for a moment I felt awash in guilt. I wanted to reel my words back in.

I confessed to God all of my fears about happiness. I wondered aloud if I was being selfish with all this happiness talk. My prayer went something like this: "God, I want to be happy. But I don't even know if I should want that! Do you care about our happiness? Is it okay for a woman who loves Jesus to desire happiness? Should I only want joy? Is happiness the reverse of holiness? Do I dare ask for happiness when I have a thousand reasons to be happy already?"

I asked God the kinds of questions that you might have

asked when you opened this book. I stood at the window, wondering if I had offended God.

But in that moment, I did not experience the condemnation of God. I felt his presence through the gift of a tender memory. My mind rewound to a season in my life when I had experienced the deepest happiness I had ever known. It was ten years earlier—the winter of 2005. After struggling with my faith, I attended a three-day women's retreat with a girlfriend. It was like Bible camp for big people. We even slept in bunk beds, and I brought my Smurf bedsheets.

That weekend, I fell in love with Jesus all over again. The concept of grace was delivered in such a fresh way that I came to know Jesus at a deeper level than I ever had before. I met women who had a passion for Jesus that was made real in their everyday lives. Scripture came alive for me. Quietly, in my top bunk one night, I rededicated my life to the Lord.

When I returned home from that retreat, none of my life circumstances had changed—but I had. I didn't choose to be happy. But I definitely *was*.

For many months after that retreat, I would wake up with a Christian worship song in my head: "Blessed Be Your Name." Before I saw the clock, my radio-mind was playing that song. It didn't matter what my day held; I knew that Jesus held me. During those tender days, I was so happy I could cry. And sometimes I did cry, out of pure delight.

But over the years, the songs in my head stopped playing. The happiness dulled. I wasn't delighting in God, or in his gifts, like I once had.

Then, many years later, I found myself at the kitchen window, where you see me now: praying for happiness and wondering if

I'd just asked for the most selfish thing in all the earth. But God didn't scold me. He had given me a fresh memory of the happiest season of my life. It was the time when I felt closest to him.

This is what he showed me: My happiness was not *apart* from him. It was *a part* of him.

My happiness all those years ago was not *separate* from my holiness. It was 100 percent entwined with it.

My happiness wasn't the reverse of joy. It was hemmed *into* my joy.

This was the beginning of the dare.

Would I dare to return to him, my first love, the source of the happiest season I'd ever experienced? Would I take a Happiness Dare?

I said yes.

The Sweet Spot of Happiness

The dare started with that one simple prayer, the first step on a wild ride that has felt like a safari of the soul. I've seen what I didn't see before—and I didn't even have to leave my regular life to find it.

The taking of the dare started, of course, in Scripture. I had to know if God was okay with happiness, if Jesus was a happy man, if happiness was counter to holiness, and if happiness was the evil cousin of joy. I needed permission to enter into a holy pursuit of happiness. I discovered that the Bible is a treasure trove of happiness. This book only touches the surface of what Scripture has to say about happiness and its synonyms.

Hear Jesus say these words over you: "I have told you this to make you as completely happy as I am" (John 15:11, CEV).

Happiness isn't
apart from God.
It is a part
of him.

The research behind the Happiness Dare didn't end there. Jesus' words whetted my appetite for more. My husband thought he might have to take out a small loan to pay for all the happiness books I bought in the year that followed. I took those books with me everywhere—to the carpool lane, to the northwoods, to a beach vacation, on airplanes while traveling to speaking engagements.

I have engrossed myself in the study of happiness.

For a year, I set a Google alert for *happiness*, which meant that nearly every news article about the subject ended up in my in-box. I read them all—literally hundreds of articles about happiness, along with dozens of books and loads of scientific research.

Why am I telling you all of this? Because if you are going to take a dare like this, you need to know that it is based on more than some willy-nilly idea of a farm wife in northwest Iowa. I have built this dare on the scaffolding of the words of Jesus. Furthermore, this dare is built by relying on the support beams of contemporary theologians and the spiritual giants of our past. These are people like John Piper, Joni Eareckson Tada, Randy Alcorn, Corrie ten Boom, Hannah Whitall Smith, C. S. Lewis, Thomas Brooks, Augustine, Charles Spurgeon, and many more.

I was given permission to be happy and I read voraciously on the topic, but my exploration didn't stop there. I still had questions. If God wants us to be happy, how do we get it? Does happiness arrive like a pizza at the front door? Do we pursue it, wait for it, or manufacture it?

I began to talk to other people about how they found happiness, and I discovered wide-ranging ideas on what happiness looks like. For some, it was the satisfaction of completing a good day's work. For others, it was having a day *off* from work.

For some, it was the joy of hosting a dinner party for a dozen friends on a Saturday night. For others, it was a merciful night of solitude.

Such variety!

Last June, I was flying to a speaking engagement in Tennessee. At 30,000 feet above ground, I pulled out my journal and began to list dozens of God-approved ways that we seek happiness. The list included things such as:

Taking in the beauty at 30,000 feet
Dark chocolate
The completion of an important assignment
A good book
Campfires
The way you feel after a good workout
The unexpected blessing of seeing God's hand on a
   hard day
An actual letter in the actual mailbox
Air guitar to '80s rock
The laundry, all folded and put away at last!
Netflix marathons
Scott's hand in mine
Committing a random act of kindness
New *Napoleon Dynamite* pajama pants
A just-on-time phone call from a dear friend
Getting snowed in

The list went on for pages.

Looking at the long list, I saw five major patterns of happiness emerging—five styles, if you will. I began to wonder how

God wired each of us to experience happiness in this world. I thought about how my idea of happiness might look different from yours. Neither idea was wrong—just different. Through this exploration, I uncovered five happiness styles, outlined in detail in the next several chapters.

This is what I now know: Happiness is found by looking closer than we dare imagine—right inside us, where the Holy Spirit lives. Each of us has a God-designed sweet spot of happiness already set within us.

I have created a diagram to help you begin to visualize your own sweet spot of happiness. Your sweet spot is the place where these three elements intersect: earthly pleasure, heavenly joy, and your unique wiring.

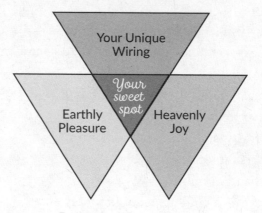

Earthly pleasure is the enjoyment we experience in the God-given gifts of the created world. The variety of those gifts is immeasurable—the starry host, the extra hour of sleep, the cup of Earl Grey, fleece-lined leggings, steak on the grill, communication by emoji, the way one sounds a bit like Taylor Swift when one is singing in the shower.

Heavenly joy is the delight and glory that our happy God experiences in his happy heaven, right now. Heavenly joy relies on the truth that God is happy, not cantankerous, and that he happily created us for his pleasure and his purposes.

Your unique wiring is an important piece of finding your sweet spot of happiness. This is how God designed you. You have a certain happiness style. (The five happiness styles are the basis for part 2 of *The Happiness Dare*. Taking the "What's Your Happiness Style?" assessment will help you find your style and learn how to maximize happiness in the life you've been given.)

In the diagram, note how all three parts intersect: earthly pleasure, heavenly joy, and your unique wiring. That place in the middle is your sweet spot. That is "Thy happy Kingdom come." When you're in your happiness sweet spot, you'll find the places, relationships, and activities that give you the greatest sense of well-being. Beware: if you veer too far toward earthly pleasure on the left—abusing God's gifts or using them to excess—you are in danger of sin and idolatry. Now, you can try to stretch as far as possible toward God's heavenly joy, but in truth, you are unable to reach that pinnacle until you arrive at the gates of heaven. Certain surprises of pure happiness will just have to wait!

Until that great day, here we are, on earth. God is calling us to live inside that sweet spot—the place in the middle. That is where we find happiness in a tangible, life-changing, holy way.

Will You Take the Dare?

Now it's your turn.

The Happiness Dare is a new beginning.

This dare is a courageous journey toward the sweet spot of

your deepest, holiest, and most vulnerable desire. I want that for myself. I want that for my husband and our children. I want that for the people I love in my everyday life.

I want that for you.

What do you say? Takers of the Happiness Dare learn that God not only cares about our happiness; he encourages us to go after it. The Happiness Dare is a challenge to enter into a holy pursuit of happiness, to boycott cynicism, to wring the delight out of ordinary days, and to hunt for happiness even when it's hard to see. And The Happiness Dare Manifesto on page 48 is your opportunity to accept the invitation.

Dare takers believe that our happiness actually matters to God. We dare takers believe that because of Jesus we have great power within us to influence our lives and the lives of others in significant ways by pursuing happiness with abandon.

Can we do this together? Can we hold one another up and promise not to compare our happiness levels? Can we allow ourselves the space to cry too? Can we remind one another that, even on the unhappiest of days, God still loves us and sees us? There's room for you on the back of the lion. There's room for more!

We need to help each other know it deep: Our happiness is an inheritance, not an illusion. It is a gift from God. He is daring us to believe something really big, and he has something so special to show us.

I'm in. I can't stop now. I know just enough to be dangerous, and I have to see what's around the bend. I will ride on the back of the lion, straight past my fears and into an enduring happiness that extends all the way to heaven.

My prayer is that once we reach the last page of this book,

we will have a whole new outlook on how to live a happy life. I pray that we will be different people, empowered by our happiness, not afraid of it.

We can dare to believe this together: Happiness is not only permissible by God but achievable through him. Happiness is our birthright. It is the holy fuel of our personhood, enabling us to live as the best versions of ourselves.

That's the secret the Holy Spirit has been whispering to me. He has been daring me to believe that happy matters. Happiness is one of the best things we can do for ourselves, for our people, and for our God. Let's believe that God is paying attention, right now, and that he has given us everything we need to live happier lives, a power that many of us have yet to unleash.

It's something that I had been walking around the edges of for years—spiritually blindfolded—and I was *so close* to finding it. God has been untying the blindfold. I am seeing what I couldn't see before. Can I show you? Look, I'm not a know-it-all here. I am still at the beginning of my expedition toward happiness, and I need you with me. See me shaking!

Quite honestly, this expedition feels subversive. I am a type-A, by-the-book, rule-following Jesus Girl. But I stepped through a door. On the inside of this journey, I feel like a rule-breaking rebel. I am a rebel against the standard rhetoric that "God doesn't care about your happiness." I am a rebel against the pious notion that happiness is a selfish ambition. I am a rebel with a cause, for Jesus. I get the feeling that, with Jesus, we will stumble upon happiness in unconventional and upside-down places, because that's the way he rolls. He was a rebel to every standard convention of the day: whom he ate with, how he traveled from place to place, how he died, and of course, how he made his unforgettable encore when he rose from the dead. Jesus is the original subversive.

This book is an invitation into a rebellious hunt that will lead you to a soul cache. I believe the Holy Spirit is saying to each of us, "Pay attention. Savor the life God has given to you. Thank God for the good when life is beautiful. And fight hard to find the happy when life is brutal."

We live in an age of cynicism, you know. And it's tempting to join the chorus of negativity. The cynics will tell us that we're being naive and silly when we talk about stalking happiness. But positive thinking and happiness are not signs of weakness. They are signs of our strength. Sometimes being joyful and grateful are the hardest, strongest things we can do in hard times. Happiness can change the world, but first it has to change us. We can't give to the world what we don't already have.

Let's do this. Let's be the happy rebels. Let's be the lion riders. Let's be the savorers and the tasters and the joy stalkers. Let's embrace a way of life where we wake up to the present-tense moments, unafraid of what might happen tomorrow and untethered to the junk that happened yesterday. Right now, this instant, life is a path strewn with jewels, glistening as if they were moonbeams spilling out like diamonds on a lake. Do we see the sparkle under our feet and on the water?

Life will hand you lemons, someone once said. And that it will. It will hand you lemons and scars and broken engagements and cancer and dandruff and orthodontia. Some of us will lose our keys, some of us will lose our hair, some of us will lose our kids at Target—and we'll all lose our ever-lovin' minds before this ride is over. There's no way around the lemons. Jesus said so: "In this world you will have trouble" (John 16:33).

Yeah, life will hand you lemons. But life will also hand you honey. And it will hand you hammocks and Netflix and queso and scarlet-red lipstick. It will hand you stolen kisses, newborn babies, peppermint candy, Silly String, elastic waistbands, clean sheets, a husband's forgiveness, and a candle in the sanctuary on Christmas Eve. It will smell like a campfire and taste like triple-fudge ice cream.

There's happiness right where we are. God is daring us to stalk it. Sometimes it shows up small. But it's important that we look, because some days the looking will save us.

Let's do this. Let's frighten the critics and baffle the cynics. Be like Jesus.

Take the dare.

Digging Deeper • • • • • • • • • • • • • • • •

1. Describe a time in your life when you were the happiest. In what ways was that happiness entwined with an awareness of God's love for you?

2. Your sweet spot of happiness is that place where three elements intersect: earthly pleasure, heavenly joy, and your unique wiring. Think about the areas of your life where you experience heavenly joy through the pleasures of this world, and through the way God has uniquely wired you.

3. How difficult is it to take the Happiness Dare in an age of cynicism, terror, and heartbreak? Why is it important to take the dare anyway?

The Happiness Dare Manifesto

Today, I am taking the dare. I have made my choice. I refuse to join the chorus of negativity. I resist the pull toward bitterness. I will not sleepwalk through my own life. I was made for more.

I accept the challenge to enter into a holy pursuit of happiness, to boycott cynicism, to wring the delight out of ordinary days, and to hunt for happiness even when it's hard to see.

I will choose happiness—because my happiness matters to God. I believe in a happy Savior who delights in my delight.

I believe that life doesn't have to be perfect to be fulfilling. I will stop wishing for the happiness in someone else's life—and discover happiness in the one I'm living. If I am trying to be like someone else, it had better be Jesus.

I won't be captivated by store-bought happiness, possessions, status, or position. Happiness is not in things; it is in me—because that's where the Holy Spirit resides.

I understand that happiness is more than a feeling; it's a decision I get to make every day.

Even though I choose happiness, I refuse to shame myself for feeling sad. I will allow myself the space to weep and mourn. And I will give other people the space to do the same.

I will look for happiness even when it's hard to find. Sometimes the looking is what will save me. Some days, this will take effort, so I pledge to make happiness a spiritual discipline.

When I choose happiness, I am not denying the pain of this world. I am refusing to give in to it.

I will choose happiness over grumpiness, because cranky Christians make horrible advertisements for Jesus.

I am committed to finding the sweet spot of my heart's deepest, holiest, and most vulnerable desire—not only for my own delight, but supremely for God's.

To Jesus Christ my Savior, thank you for showing me what happiness is. Of all the people in the world, your followers should be the happiest of all. Let my life reveal that truth. I will honor you, from this day forward, in my holy pursuit of happiness.

I'm in.

Signed: _____

Date: _____

PART 2

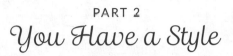

You Have a Style

In this section of *The Happiness Dare*, we will:

Discover the five happiness styles and learn how God
already wired us for happiness right where we are

Let go of the idea that our own happiness style
has to look like someone else's

Stop wishing for someone else's life and discover
happiness in the one we have

Learn how to boost the happiness of our family
and friends by understanding their personal
happiness styles

Understand what "happiness shaming" is
and learn how to avoid suffering from it
—or inflicting it on others

CHAPTER 4

The Importance of Finding Your Happiness Style

⤳

Where your pleasure is, there is your treasure; where your treasure is, there is your heart; where your heart is, there is your happiness.

AUGUSTINE

Something wonderful happened to my daughter Lydia during seventh grade.

Lo, a more unbelievable sentence has never been written in a book. Because there are two words that—when juxtaposed—strike fear in the hearts of men and women everywhere: *junior high.*

How many people do you know who claim, "I totally owned junior high. Those were the happiest years of my life"? Sources say the answer is approximately zero people.

I still suffer from anxiety when I walk down Lydia's junior high hallway. When I visit Lydia's school, my mind sometimes snaps back to my own junior high days. I remember, for instance, the embarrassment of shooting a basketball and actually scoring for the first time all season—for the wrong team.

My legs and arms were the approximate circumference of lolli-pop sticks. My hair had its own zip code. I had the coordination of a baby giraffe on roller skates.

So indeed, the first sentence of this chapter requires the reader to willingly suspend disbelief. But stick with me here: Junior high has something important to teach us all about the art of happy living, the joy-killing ritual of comparison, and the way we're uniquely wired by God to experience happiness in our lives.

Comparison Robs Us of Our Happiness

In the interest of full disclosure, Lydia's seventh-grade year started out rough.

There were frustrations over friendships and the great "Who's Who of the Seventh Grade"—determined almost universally by one's dexterity in dodgeball.

Many cheerless nights, she and I lay beside each other on her bed, staring at the ceiling with our fingers laced behind our heads. The darkness couldn't conceal the anguish of a kid trying to figure out who she was, nor could it hide a mother's helpless tears. I was desperate to help my daughter navigate the treachery of junior high. Self-discovery is hard work.

Lydia saw what made her friends happy: sports. So she joined the school's basketball team. Her best friends were star athletes; meanwhile, Lydia was one of the last ones to come off the bench. On nights before basketball games, Lydia and I would pray for "just one basket"—and that she'd one-up her old mom by scoring said basket for her own team. This, we thought, would make her happy.

In the dead of winter, Lydia's team's final game of the season was about to begin. Lydia still hadn't scored a basket. Everyone on the team and on our side of the bleachers knew it.

In the second quarter, the coach called Lydia off the bench and into the game. The girls ran up and down the court, trying their best to defend against a team of highly skilled Dutch-ancestry girls—a small army of blonde giants wearing red jerseys.

Just before the halftime buzzer, Lydia caught a pass and shot the ball into the air. The ball circled the rim, and then that barbaric orb dropped to the side. Crestfallen, Lydia slumped back to the locker room with her teammates. Never in the history of halftime bleacher-hood has a mother prayed harder for a basket to be made.

By the time the game entered the fourth quarter, the chance for an answered prayer had dimmed. The coach put my girl in one final time, bless her heart. Lydia looked up into the stands. I gave her my thumbs-up and a smile that tried to say a hundred things at once: *I love you! I believe in you! Your shoe's untied! You will survive if you don't make a basket!*

Red numbers blinked back from the scoreboard's timer. 1:30, 1:29, 1:28. Time was running out.

One of the star players on Lydia's team ended up with the ball, dribbled three times, and got trapped behind two of the giants near the free-throw line. Lydia scooted around the red jerseys and spread her fingers wide. Several girls from the bench yelled, "Get it to Lydia! She's open!" One of Lydia's teammates bounce-passed to her.

Lydia dribbled, sliding miraculously through the blurred red of the giants. It was the parting of a modern-day Red Sea. The ball flicked off the end of Lydia's fingertips and sailed upward.

The ball circled mercilessly on the hoop, while a long bleacher full of mamas tilted in their seats—to the left and then to the right—as if we could alter the effects of gravity to force that one ball through the hoop. The screech of shoe soles on the gym floor stopped. Everyone froze in place.

Then it happened: With 00:59 left on the clock—*swish*—Lydia scored a basket.

I have no idea who won the game, now that I think of it; I was simply so thrilled for my girl. When Lydia got home, I met her at the back door, wrapped her up in a hug, and congratulated her.

Let's push the pause button on this story. I know what you might be thinking. You might assume that I'm going to tell you Lydia found happiness because of her perseverance. But that isn't what I'm going to tell you. This wasn't the moment she found happiness. *This was the moment when she found herself.* The happiness would come later.

Our story continues at the back door.

"Lydia!" I gushed. "I'm so happy for you!"

She shrugged. "Thanks, Mom. I guess."

"What do you mean, 'I guess'?" I clucked. "This is what we prayed for, what you've been working toward all season. Didn't you see how happy your teammates were for you? Weren't you thrilled?"

"Yeah. But no. It was really nice, but . . ." Her voice trailed off. "It was actually embarrassing, Mom. Because everyone was so excited, and it was like a scene in a movie where the whole crowd feels sorry for one kid who finally gets to make the big play. I really *was* happy to make a basket, but you know? Basketball isn't my thing. It makes my friends happy, but it doesn't make me happy."

I was half a second away from talking her out of everything she'd said. But then I re-remembered what I had re-forgotten. The truth had slipped away from me for a moment, despite the fact that I had repeated it hundreds of times in blog posts, on conference stages, and in bedtime conversations with our two daughters.

This is the truth I remembered: We can stop trying to be someone we're not.

Happiness begins in that moment when we look within and say, "I was not created to be her. I was created to be me."

Happiness really is an inside job. You don't find happiness by being the best version of someone else. You find happiness by being the best version of you.

Lydia discovered this earlier than many of us, but what's true in junior high is also true on cul-de-sacs, in church sanctuaries, and in the corporate high-rise where you work. What brings your best friend happiness might make you break out in hives. Your hyper-state of happiness at an amusement park might seem one inch shy of cuckoo town to your sister. The fact that you are happy at your job might baffle your friends who would rather spend the afternoon thrift shopping.

What brings us happiness varies widely. There are moms who actually enjoy hosting Pinterest-perfect half-birthday parties for their cats. There are couples who delight in lakeside picnics and others who hate the itchy grass. Some people delight in tidying up their houses and completing small tasks, like washing the dishes. If that's you, by all means: Do it! (And then come over to my house.)

Happiness really can be found in the little things. It's that contented sigh when you cross the last item off the to-do list.

It's the morning's first cup of coffee. It's the smile you get when you drop off a loaf of still-warm banana bread for your elderly neighbor. It's the sound of your friend's laughter, and you realize she got the punch line before you even said it. It's a clean floor, an organized pantry, the scent of a freshly bathed baby. It's the anticipation you feel as you drive to your book club, wondering whether your friends made the same discoveries you did. Happiness may be a night curled up on the couch with your husband, two hands touching in the popcorn bowl as you watch Shark Week. Maybe for you, happiness is a night on the back deck, under the stars, while a coyote howls in the distance.

There is no one way to happiness. In Jesus, there are uncountable ways.

Think what it would mean for each of us if we learned where we are happiest of all. Think if we could discover our own styles of happiness and then multiply what brings us joy. Think how it could change our moments, our days, our homes, our workplaces. Our lives.

Remember: When our happiness increases in manifold, God-honoring ways, we are not being selfish or sinful. The happier we are, the more we are becoming like our Savior.

Before he went to the Cross, Jesus gave us a road map for happiness, and he said we would find it by remaining in his love, like branches joined to a vine. "I have told you this to make you as completely happy as I am," Jesus told the disciples.[1]

God wired us for happiness, not to make us heretics but to make us holy. It's time to discover how God designed you, to uncover the places where greater happiness awaits you like unwrapped gifts from your Father.

It's time to do what Flannery O'Connor did: to stalk joy as if it can change things.

Because it can.

It's All in Your Wiring

When I took my Happiness Dare, I began to explore whether God had wired people uniquely for happiness. I knew that the Bible revealed how God's people are given an array of individual talents and spiritual gifts. And I could see that in my own circle of friends and relatives. God is so creative!

The diversity in the body of Christ has been so liberating for me. Not all of us are called to be basketball players or cake bakers or undertakers. That means that I don't have to kill it in everything. I'm called to excellence in my own square foot of space on earth. The same goes for you.

Every part of the body has a purpose. Every eyelash, every fingernail, every elbow, every funny bone. In the body of Christ, there is no such thing as an appendix. No part is excisable, wasted, or useless. This is why some of us end up as overseas missionaries while others of us end up as schoolteachers, interior designers, janitors, or stay-at-home parents.

"As it is," the apostle Paul wrote, "we see that God has carefully placed each part of the body right where he wanted it."[2] Paul had a lot more to say about that. "Now God gives us many kinds of special abilities," Paul wrote, "but it is the same Holy Spirit who is the source of them all."[3]

One God; many kinds of abilities. *The Message* paraphrases it like this: "The variety is wonderful."[4]

I began to wonder if the following was also true: One God; many kinds of *happiness*. Was it possible, with regard to happiness, that "the variety is wonderful"?

A caveat here: I am not equating happiness styles to spiritual gifts. But God's originality in creating individuals with unique gifts has caused me to pause and ask questions about how he has built us to experience happiness in wide-ranging ways. We are not clones in our jobs. We are not clones with our talents. We are not clones with our spiritual gifts. Why, then, would we be clones in happiness?

According to stories in Scripture, people find happiness in manifold ways. The variety is indeed wonderful! Open the pages of Scripture to discover happiness pouring out: an old woman finds out she's pregnant; a blind man sees for the first time ever; a whole generation is delivered to a new land; a dude who was dead for four days walks out of his tomb; a guy named David dances so giddily that people think he's lost it. Find people enthralled in their worship and also in their work. Consider the probable joy of Bezalel and Oholiab, gifted craftsmen who were tapped to help with the Tabernacle. I wonder how happy the early Christian Tabitha must have felt when she was helping the poor. I cannot imagine Barnabas being a malcontent. Chances are he was a happy encourager, not a grumpy one.[5]

Happiness can be found all over the Bible and in a million places on earth this very minute, but the source of all authentic happiness is closer than we dared dream.

The source? "Christ in you."[6]

Happiness isn't in things. It isn't in places. It isn't in vacations. It isn't reserved only for heaven. Happiness is in us. Right now. Christ dwells inside each of us.

But the Spirit inside us doesn't make us clones. He makes us sisters and brothers.

Happiness Is Not One-Size-Fits-All

For Lydia, junior high changed when she realized that she wasn't made for the basketball court. Instead, she was made for the band room.

At the end of her seventh-grade year, Lydia discovered her love and talent for music while playing in the concert band and singing in the junior high musical. She uncovered natural gifts in playing the clarinet, the marimba, the piano, and more.

That's when she learned: For some, happiness was found on the basketball court. But for her, it was in the music room. She was the happiest I had seen her in months.

When Lydia is making music, she shines. She loses herself. In those moments, I see my girl in a hyperfocused state of sublime happiness. The piano bench is my daughter's sweet spot—the place where earthly pleasure, heavenly joy, and her unique wiring intersect.

Just before her eighth-grade year began, Lydia decided to focus on her sweet spots. She decided she wasn't going to join the basketball team. She would devote more time to band, choir, and the school's dramatic productions. It was as if Lydia had received a happiness transplant.

This is a good place to tell you that Scott and I do not condone quitting clubs or teams that we've already signed up for. We regularly encourage each other to take on new challenges. Like her mother, Lydia is a type-A perfectionist, and it takes a lot of spiritual pep-talking for people like us to try something new, especially if we think we might fail. That's part of the reason Lydia joined the cross-country team last fall. All people ought to do something that feels a little scary. Failure isn't fatal. Often it's fruitful because it shows you what you're made of when you get back up again. God cares greatly about our character, and sometimes that sort of character development will make us a bit uncomfortable.

But as much as we shouldn't shy away from trying new things, we shouldn't feel guilty if we redirect ourselves toward our happiness sweet spots—the places where God wired us to find authentic happiness in him. We have permission to be the people God created us to be.

It is easier to find that sweet spot than we dared imagine. And it starts by living as the best versions of ourselves.

Can I confess something? I've lived otherwise. Several years ago, I befriended a group of women who loved scrapbooking. Up until that point of my life, I had been feeling pretty proud that my photos were in actual shoe boxes, stacked together in one closet.

Then I began paging through the thick photo albums on their coffee tables, admiring the creatively cut photos of their children. The scrapbook pages were themed: beach day, circus day, first haircut, field trip. Photos were lined with borders. Pages were decorated with cute, shiny stickers. Every image was accompanied by a paragraph description, written in gold-star penmanship.

After I complimented one of my friends on her album, she clapped her hands together and said, "You should come to my scrapbooking party! It's super fun!"

I shook my head and told her I didn't have the albums, tools, or creativity to put together a scrapbook. I told her how I stored my photos in boxes.

Her eyes widened, big as drink coasters. She told me about the damage that awaited my photos. She used words like *archival paper* and *oval cutting system*. She made me believe that my photos would disintegrate into dust within 3.2 years. *She had just the products for me!*

One hour and $375 later, I was the proud owner of a leather-bound photo album, an oval cutting system, some fancy scissors, and a pile of stickers. I accepted the invitation to her scrapbook party the following week.

I showed up that night with all of my tools, along with hundreds of photographs. (If nothing else, I was ambitious.) I set everything out, drummed my fingers on the table, and wondered, *Now what?*

I fought with the cutter and chopped off a baby's head. I smudged the ink on my carefully crafted paragraphs. All around the room, other women had entered a sublime state of scrapbooking bliss, creating page after page. I kept thinking, *I should be* enjoying *this. This is what women do. What's wrong with me?*

Years later, I realized that there wasn't anything wrong with me at all. Scrapbooking, as it turns out, makes me the opposite of happy. I would actually prefer a night watching a documentary with my kids, making a gourmet dinner with my husband, or jotting notes in a journal for the next day's blog post. I take great joy in all of those moments because that's how God wired me.

On the basketball court and at the scrapbooking party, Lydia and I did what many people do. We looked at what made others happy and made these assumptions about ourselves:

1. If I want to be happy, I need to do what they're doing.
2. I would be happier if I were made like they're made.

We wrongly assume that happiness comes in a one-size-fits-all package. But the truth is, our capacity for happiness was designed by God, not by us.

Just as we were created to bring glory to God with our unique spiritual gifts, we are also wired to bring him glory through our own unique style of happiness. If you've been tirelessly hunting for your happiness somewhere "out there," this is liberating news!

You can stop wishing for the happiness of someone else's life—and discover happiness in the one you have. If you trust that God is a happy God who happily made us, you can trust that he has given you everything you need to find the sweet spot of your heart's deepest desire.

Like Lydia and me, you could waste months or years enviously cataloging the happy lives of others. You could waste precious hours of life comparing their talents to your lack of ability. You could walk blindly past your own happiness sweet spots every day while never really stopping to nourish them.

Or you could get on with the business of rediscovering who you really are as a way of uncovering a new, rich vision of happiness.

The Five Styles of Happiness

This is where it gets exciting for all of us.

When I took this Happiness Dare, I began to explore my theory that God uniquely wired us for happiness. I tested that theory by interviewing people from ages eleven to ninety-two. We talked about what made them happiest. The variety was, indeed, wonderful. Then I asked some psychologists, ministry leaders, and counselors to help me understand the varied ways people experience contentment and joy in life. I read hundreds of news articles, clinical studies, and works of scientific research that examined happiness. I then created an assessment tool to see if we could pinpoint people's individual styles. Over the next several months, many of my friends, family members, and ministry partners, as well as other book authors, agreed to take the test and offer feedback. The findings were eye-opening and affirming for people, providing useful information for them to use when nourishing their own sweet spots of happiness.

After much research and testing, I concluded that there are five major determinants of happiness. They are:

- Believing that one's life has purpose
- Having a sense of belonging
- Culling happiness from moments and experiences
- Helping others feel loved and cherished
- Using the power of our minds to learn, plan, and dream

Based on these five determinants, I identified five happiness styles:

 The Doers: Doers find supreme happiness in purposeful activity. They are in their happy place when they are doing what they were created to do—and doing it well.

The Relaters: Relaters find supreme happiness in positive, meaningful relationships with others. They thrive in the company of friends and family.

 The Experiencers: Experiencers find supreme happiness by engaging in meaningful moments with a sense of adventure, curiosity, and whimsy—at home or on the road.

 The Givers: Givers find supreme happiness by seeking ways to bring delight to others. They believe that a shared happiness is a double happiness.

 The Thinkers: Thinkers find supreme happiness in the contemplative work of the mind. They take delight in learning, pondering, and dreaming.

Can you already guess which one you are? Because you are uniquely wired, you will most likely find that you naturally flourish in some areas more than others.

I know people of all five happiness types. Many of those people also have clear secondary subtypes, and you may find that you do as well. It has been terrifically thrilling to help people I know discover where they come most alive with happiness.

Volumes of research back up these five personal styles of happiness. Get this: So does Scripture. The Bible calls us to a full life that engages all of the happiness styles.

In the pages that follow, you will find out where you flourish. You will learn how to maximize your happiness based on how God made you by taking the happiness style assessment.

You'll gain insights on how to create happy places for the people in your life whose happiness styles differ from yours. Understanding your happiness style will help you learn how to interpret your feelings and responses toward others.

You'll learn that no matter what style is wired into you, you have the ability to maximize your happiness through three different types of happiness:

- **Anticipatory happiness** occurs when you are looking forward to what makes you happy (for example, as you plan a vacation).

- **In-the-moment happiness** is experienced in real time (for example, as you take the vacation you planned).

- **Residual happiness** is created when you remember what made you happy in the past (for example, as you recall memories of the vacation you took months or years ago).

In the pages that follow, you'll also learn how to see warning signs that your personal happiness is becoming an idol. Like all good things, even legitimate sources of happiness and pleasure can turn toxic if they are elevated above God.

No Happiness Shaming Allowed

Friend, you will find freedom here. Whether you love scrapbooking, random acts of kindness, or Silly String on a Saturday morning. Whether you find happiness in your office or whether you prefer a snuggle on the sofa.

This is a shame-free zone. As takers of the Happiness Dare, we pledge not to participate in what I call "happiness shaming." Happiness shaming is what happens when we lay guilt trips on others (or on ourselves) because we find happiness in different pursuits. Happiness shaming also occurs when people feel (or inflict) guilt over delighting in some experience or thing. We do not need to despise the pleasures of the world. We are called to enter into right relationship with them. There is no shame in enjoying the gifts that God has given us. Maybe we all need to know this:

Happiness in God is not limited to quiet time.
Just because you're smiling doesn't mean you're sinning.

God gave us the created world—with sugar, bluebirds, audio books, Words with Friends, art museums, and sex. You have permission to enjoy food, friendship, and a cool swim on a hot day. The devil didn't make art, laughter, music, or Sunday afternoon naps. God did!

God made a physical world not so you would fear it or despise it, but so you might draw nearer to him *through* it.

Of course, we worship the Giver, not the gifts. With a hand raised to the sky, I pledge that we should bow before God alone, not to the stuff he makes for us. But as John Calvin wrote, "In despising the gifts, we insult the Giver."[7] And in embracing the gifts, we honor the Giver, because he is the one who gave them. As the apostle James writes, "Every good thing given and every perfect gift is from above, coming down from the Father of lights."[8]

Look, if you are in Jesus, you probably aren't reading this

book in a selfish pursuit of happiness. You know that happiness is not a me-only pursuit divorced from God. You've seen how self-centered happiness can become an exercise in excess. As we pursue happiness, we can hold one another accountable so that we maximize our happiness in a way that honors and glorifies the Giver.

If you still aren't convinced, you're free to leave now—but only if you can say the following statement with a straight face: "I don't want to be happy."

Oh, good. You're still here. Whew. Can I tell you how relieved I am? We need you. We need your own style of happiness. Together, this dare is going to change us. And then it will change our world.

Imagine how our happiness can help us witness to a world in need of the gospel. Imagine how the world might see the elevated happiness that people can experience only in Jesus. All people were created by God and have access to his gifts in the natural world, which means that even unbelievers can taste happiness. But because we are in Jesus, our happiness ought to be increased tenfold! We have the love of a Savior, the hope of a resurrection, and the promise of God's presence and peace *right now*.

Miserable Christians make horrible public-relations agents for the gospel. Imagine a world where our happy lives illustrate an attractive gospel. The Good News is a heritage of happiness. When we maximize our happiness, other people notice. They want what we have. Authentic happiness can change our world.

But first it has to change us.

I am not talking about chasing the next thrill, the smaller size, or the perfect color for your front door. I am talking about extracting something that God has planted inside you to cultivate and to grow, so you can become the fullest version of yourself.

I dare you to ask yourself these questions: *What makes me happy? What does my happiest day look like? What do others say brings life to me? What do they see in me?*

A. W. Tozer once said that the people of God "ought to be the happiest people in all the wide world! People should be coming to us constantly and asking the source of our joy and delight."[9]

Let's give them a reason to ask.

Note to reader: Before you read any further, take five minutes to learn your own happiness style by taking the happiness style assessment. The easiest way to take the assessment is to visit us online at www.thehappinessdare.com. The assessment is also found on page 269 of this book.

Chances are you will have one dominant happiness style that stands out from the rest. Most of us also have secondary happiness styles. You'll know your secondary style when you look at your second-highest score. Do not be alarmed if you score similarly across more than one happiness style.

Knowing your dominant personal style(s) will reveal a lot about you. It will help you experience God's purpose and delight in your life more than ever before.

Digging Deeper ● ● ● ● ● ● ● ● ● ● ● ● ● ● ● ● ● ●

1. On page 57, Jennifer writes, "You don't find happiness by being the best version of someone else. You find happiness by being the best version of you." How have you found that to be true in your own life?

2. Jennifer tells a story about attending a scrapbooking party and how she assumed there was something wrong with her because she didn't enjoy what the other women enjoyed. Have you ever felt weird or shamed because your idea of happiness didn't fit in a neat little box of what happiness is supposed to look like? Explain.

3. A. W. Tozer said that the people of God "ought to be the happiest people in all the wide world." Are we? Why or why not?

4. How did the results of the happiness style assessment make you feel? Were they what you expected? Why or why not?

CHAPTER 5

The Doer

⌣

My Father never stops working, and so I keep working, too.

JESUS IN JOHN 5:17, NCV

So you're a Doer, are you? (Even if you're not a Doer, read along. Chances are, you know several Doers, and understanding their happiness styles will help you understand and love them better. Plus, we all can learn from each other!)

Welcome to the club of the goal setters, the task jugglers, and the people who happily get 'er done.

As a Doer, you find supreme happiness in purposeful activity. You are happiest when you are doing what you were created to do—and when you are doing it well.

Some people go to the beach in search of happiness. Some curl up with a good book by the fire. Some linger over coffee with close friends. You might also enjoy beaches and books, but as a Doer, few things make you happier than being productive.

You don't wait for the weekend to create the happy life God intended for you. You are building a life from which you don't need a vacation.

You are a person of many layers, so not every characteristic of a Doer will fit you perfectly. But people tend to describe you as *determined* and *dependable*, and this makes you happy.

What Makes You Tick

You love: a good day's work. As thankful as you are when the clock strikes five on a Friday afternoon, you can be ridiculously jubilant at eight o'clock on a Monday morning. You love completing the tasks set before you. Those assignments might take you to a cubicle or a conference room, but they are also the kinds of duties that keep a home running, the lawn mowed, a table set, presents wrapped, and invitations mailed. In short, you are a modern-day Martha.[1]

If you had tomorrow afternoon free: you would most enjoy it by being productive in tasks at home, at the office, or in the yard. You are not a fun hater. To you, work is part of the fun.

You connect with God by: seeing how the earthly pleasure of daily work intersects with the heavenly joy of colaboring with God. You don't see work as a curse caused by the Fall but as a blessing from heaven.

You would be lost without: your to-do list. You're tickled pink when all the boxes have neat little Xs inside of them. Even small household chores, like emptying the dishwasher, offer a sort of residual happiness—once the tasks are finished.

Let's not wait
for the weekend
to create the
happy life that
God intended
for us.

People say you are: someone they can always count on. They call you reliable, and in fact may have asked you to lead the committee, organize the fund-raiser, or plan the party. You are purpose-driven and goal-oriented. When you set your sights on accomplishing something, it's as good as done.

If you're at a dinner party: you happily head straight for the kitchen to help the hostess. You feel out of place when the work is done and all that's left is small talk.

Red Flags for Doers

You're outside your happiness sweet spot when: you're over-indulging in work. You sometimes can't enjoy your present level of progress because you are hyperfocused on what's next. Ironically, we are all at our greatest risk of falling into sin or idolatry in the area where we are most wired to experience pleasure and happiness, so Doers have to pay attention to keeping their love of work in check.

People who aren't afraid to speak truth to you would say: you are prone to perfectionism and legalism. You sometimes believe that your worth is tied to your performances, and so you have a hard time saying no.

You can feel unsettled when: you're not completing tasks. If there's a sudden change in your ability to do work—for example, because of a job loss, retirement, or sickness—you are deflated.

You feel you've let God down when: you bungle an assignment or blow a deadline.

You feel shame when: people tell you that you are too type A, too driven, and don't take enough time for yourself. Sometimes you have secretly wished you were more Mary, less Martha, and a bit more spontaneous.

You shame others when: they fly by the seats of their pants or miss deadlines. You die a little on the inside when others waste time, don't pull their weight on a project, take breaks when tasks clearly aren't finished, or appear generally incompetent.

How to Be the Happiest You

You will be in your sweet spot when: you are consciously working alongside God, happily doing what you were created to do to make the world a better place. You can maximize your sweet spot by praying before doing your tasks. Invite Jesus into the work you're doing while folding the laundry, balancing the books, pulling weeds, hiring a new employee, sweeping crumbs, or making copies.

You will stay in your sweet spot when: you guard against workaholism and perfectionism. Because you are task-oriented, you may need to add vacation itself as an item on the to-do list. You may need to make relaxation a goal. You know that God isn't an item on a checklist, but consider adding connection with God to the top of your list so you don't lose sight of him as you happily go about your work.

Avoid shaming yourself by: realizing we are all created differently. What brings you happiness might make your Experiencer friends hyperventilate. There's nothing wrong with you if, during a beach-house vacation, you enjoy staying inside to fix a gourmet meal that everyone will love.

Avoid shaming others by: realizing they were created for their own sweet spots too. Just as they have something to learn from you, you have something to learn from the Relaters, Experiencers, Givers, and Thinkers. Like you, they were created in the image of God. Don't hassle your Experiencer friends who are making sand castles while you cook that gourmet meal.

You can love the Doers in your life by: giving them space to work and "do" when they need a happiness recharge. You can encourage them to do what brings them happiness and affirm how you see God at work in them, even as they work.

The Holy Happiness of a Doer

I am a Doer. I especially love my work as a writer. I can get playfully lost in what I'm doing right this instant—stringing together words that will eventually find their way to you.

This office is one of my happy places.

Most mornings, I walk into this room, and even though it's a bit messy, it feels like a sanctuary. Sunlight slants in through the stained-glass window. A handmade quilt is folded on the back of my chair. The computer screen stretches out like a canvas. I love to make art with words, an act of cocreating with God. I sit down in this place every day, expectant and hopeful. I pray for words—and for you. Then I get to work.

I do confess, my office is not always a happy place. There are days when writing is as painful as pulling out my eyelashes— and almost as productive. You'll know the days I have a deadline looming on a writing project. Those are the days when I tackle the pressing needs of the moment, like alphabetizing the spices or sorting my landscaping rocks by color.

Because of the nature of work, even the happiest Doers are likely to encounter moments that frustrate more than delight. Writer's block momentarily derails an author. A database error confounds the computer programmer. But Doers push through, knowing that happiness awaits them when the task is complete. That's anticipatory happiness, and overcoming those challenges also gives the Doers a happiness boost after the fact. Doers look back on the day with a sense of contentment. That's residual happiness.

I wasn't always so sure that God intended us to find work so fulfilling. I actually used to feel guilty about how much I loved my work. (Happiness shaming? I didn't need anyone else to lay that on me; I shamed myself.) Wouldn't God prefer me as a Relater, finding supreme happiness in the company of others? Or as a Giver, supremely happy when doing good deeds for my neighbor?

Part of the problem lies in our attitude toward work. I once had a pastor tell me that work was a four-letter word. And while the pastor may have been joking, there is a pervasive and stubborn myth that work is a curse. We call it the "daily grind." Of course, we all despise office politics, pointless busywork, and seasons of unending routine at the office or at home—like the clothes that always need to be put on hangers in the closet. These are very real pressures of work, and they are a result of the curse on this world. (Curse you, laundry piles!)

But work itself isn't a curse. It is not a punishment. It is, in the words of Elisabeth Elliot, a blessing. "The enjoyment of leisure would be nothing if we had only leisure. It is the *joy of work well done* that enables us to enjoy rest."[2]

In enjoying work, there is no question that we have to guard against perfectionism and workaholism. If we only work and never sit at the feet of Jesus, we will suffer from chronic spiritual atrophy. Our work will be in vain if Jesus isn't in it.

One way to safeguard against overdoing our doing is to ask ourselves these questions:

- *Is this work for the glory of God, or for the glory of me?*
- *Am I striving out of legalism or a need for control?*
- *Am I working this hard because it makes me happy, or because I grew up in a home where my worth was based on what I could do?*

Like anything in this world, our work—even ministry work—can become toxic if we elevate it above God.

But God does not despise your work. He made you for it. God is the ultimate Doer. Since the beginning of time, God has been in the business of doing. And we can surmise from Scripture that he does it quite happily.

Jesus: The Ultimate Doer

Once upon a time, God created the world that we're living in. For six days straight, he showed up at work and made stuff. He was a Doer, happily creating protozoa and polar caps, puffer fish and pansies and pelicans. How can we be so sure he was happy while breathing stars and sculpting the Cliffs of Moher? Because he declared it good. God saw what he made and took pleasure in it. A Creator who declares his work good is a Creator who is delighted. Imagine him with a smile at the end of his workday, not as some frustrated guy in middle management who shuffles out the door at five o'clock while rolling his eyes. God is a happy Doer. And he made us the same way.

On the sixth day of creation, God kicked his doing up to a whole other level. He made Adam. But before he gave Adam a mate, he gave him work. Before he gave him an outfit to wear, he gave him a job.

As Doers, we can draw great happiness from our work, knowing it brings glory to God. "Whatever you do," Paul wrote, "work at it with all your heart, as working for the Lord, not for human masters."[3]

Anywhere we work with God, we can experience his divine happiness. In God, happiness and purposeful work are a package deal. Even in the office, with its cutthroat competition and bad coffee. Even in the nursery, with its overflowing laundry hamper and constantly full Diaper Genie.

Even in the kitchen. Take it from a man who felt happiness while peeling potatoes and washing pans in a monastery kitchen four hundred years ago. Brother Lawrence, in the clatter of that kitchen, said he possessed "God in as great a tranquillity as if I were upon my knees at the blessed sacrament." (Incidentally, in that same book, we read, "What tragic misunderstanding to regard [God] as a killer of happiness!")[4]

Doers show us what it's like to draw happiness from our work. Doers take delight in making meals, writing poems, straightening teeth, x-raying broken bones, nursing babies, and even mopping floors.

My friend Carla is a housekeeper at a Christian drug and

alcohol rehab center in a nearby town. She classifies herself as a Doer. "It makes me so happy that I get to do what I do every day," she said. "The other day, one of the clients dropped her cereal on the floor, and it spilled everywhere. She started crying, and I just told her, 'Honey, you go on and get yourself another bowl of cereal. I will clean this up. I want to do that for you.' I feel like I get to take the burdens off of other people's shoulders when I go to work."

Carla says that she's not an eloquent speaker and insists that she could never be a mouthpiece for Jesus: "I can't speak for Jesus, but I can be his hands and feet. And when I'm washing floors, I feel like I'm washing feet." (I'd say she's pretty eloquent too.)

If you are a Mary, we need you and highly esteem you, and we can learn a lot from you. But if you are a Doer like Martha, you don't have to feel guilty about it. We can't be the hands and feet of Jesus unless we're actually *doing* something with them. Without Martha, Mary wouldn't have had an uncluttered place to sit. And while Jesus gently admonished Martha—and don't we all need gentle admonishment from time to time?—we don't want to forget this: "Jesus loved Martha."[5]

Yep. Our Savior loves the Doer.

The Story of a Doer

Hell hath no fury like a type-A Doer who feels that her "doing" has been found lacking. Especially by her own mother.

Mom was due for a visit.

It was right after we built our house on a gently sloping hill, framed by cornfields and domed by the hard blue sky of the heartland. It was 2002.

Our house has a big kitchen with a stone backsplash, shiny black appliances, and rustic maple planks on the floor. The windows are tall, framed in wood the color of cinnamon. In those first few weeks, I would stand in the middle of the sparsely furnished living room, close my eyes, and smell the scent of new carpet, fresh paint, and varnish.

I babied that house the way you take care of anything new. The way, when you get a new car (even if it's a new-to-you car manufactured in 2004), you freakishly obsess over every pebble, every speck of lint, every french fry that falls between the seats. Oh, you settle down over time, but at first you tend to your new thing like it's your job.

In my new house, no dust bunny went unnoticed. No crumb went unswept. No cobweb escaped my roving eyes. My house seemed perfectly spotless, and I was on cloud nine.

Mom showed up at 10 a.m. on a Tuesday.

Oh, Mother. Bless her heart. Mom is a four-foot-eleven-inch biblical Martha on steroids. I love her to pieces, but when she came to visit in those early months in our new house, I was a hot mess of anxiety.

Within the first hour of her visit, Mom merrily requested a dust rag and a can of Pledge. "Now, where do you keep your broom these days?" she asked while opening closet doors.

Baby on my hip, I walked to the nursery to change a diaper and take an adult time-out while cartoonish steam shot out my ears. I returned to find my mother folding my husband's boxers.

I can't overstate how offended I was that my mother had clearly found me in violation of her high standards of cleanliness and order. I think I still have the teeth marks in my tongue.

With each visit, I'd go through the same routine. I'd spend

days before Mom's arrival rearranging condiments in the refrigerator, removing hair from drains, and collecting coins from
under the cushions so that Mom would find me in compliance
with her housekeeping code.

Suddenly my happy place had become decidedly unhappy.
I was cleaning like a crazy person, out of pride, hoping to win
a secret war that I was waging against my own mother. We had
become dueling Doers. After multiple visits, I knew I wasn't
going to win.

And then I had a thought: What if this wasn't a contest to
be won? What if this wasn't an assault on me or my cleanliness?
What if this was just . . . Mom being Mom? Maybe she actually enjoyed rearranging my Tupperware cupboard. Maybe she
felt like she was helping her daughter, a young mom who had
moved to a new community where she didn't know anybody.

Maybe completing little tasks for me made her—*wait for
it*—happy.

I thought I'd test my new theory. Mom was coming over
to take care of the girls while we were away for the weekend.
Instead of knocking myself out by performing reconstructive
surgery on the house, I left each room in its more natural state.
I didn't dust. I left laundry in the hampers. And I made a list of
tasks that Mom could complete if she wanted to do so.

Wash basement windows.
Clean out shelves in refrigerator.
Work out the stain on the kitchen rug.

When she arrived, I handed her the list warily. What if
she reckoned me lazy? But that didn't happen at all. Her eyes

widened with joy, like I'd handed her the Good Housekeeping seal of approval.

Sure enough, my mom is a Doer. Doing purposeful work makes her happy. Furthermore, Mom is a Giver (see chapter 8), and she took delight in helping out an overwhelmed daughter.

Some people find happiness in a hammock or on a hiking trail. Give my mom a bottle of Windex and a dirty mirror, and that woman has entered a state of euphoria.

She cleans quite happily. And then, because she's made in the image of her Father, she stands back, admires the lines of the vacuum in the carpet, and declares it good.

Maximizing Our Sweet Spot, One Small Act at a Time

What does all of this mean for the Doers? And what can everyone else learn from the Doers in their lives?

All of this means that we have permission to actually enjoy our jobs, our productivity, and our accomplishments. It means that we can look for opportunities to maximize our "doing" in small ways throughout the day.

It means that if you know your job is a bad fit—if it doesn't align with the way God made you—it might be time to freshen up your résumé. Maybe you hate the job you're in, but it pays the bills, or you are recently retired, and after years of taking delight in your work, you are feeling empty and aimless. One place to begin? Devote a few minutes every day to completing small tasks that provide residual happiness—raking the neighbors' leaves or delivering a meal to a neighbor (especially if you're also a Relater or Giver; see chapters 6 and 8).

If you still don't know where to begin, start small, perhaps with a task as simple as making your bed. I'm not joking when I tell you that it can make a person happier.

So first, a confession: I stopped making my bed on a regular basis after I left home for college in 1990. (Some perspective: That's the year MC Hammer hit the charts with "U Can't Touch This.") But one April morning last year, I made my bed. I pulled the sheets tight, straightened the comforter over the top, and set the pillows just so. And because I was feeling particularly ambitious, I opened the blinds to let the morning light stream in on that tidy rectangle.

I had spent the previous quarter of a century convincing myself that making the bed was an utter waste of time, seeing how we'd only be undoing that same bed at night. This doesn't mean that I *never* made my bed during those twenty-five years. I would enthusiastically make my bed after purchasing a new bedding set at the store. But my enthusiasm would wane after approximately 37.5 hours. I also made the bed when we were expecting guests, particularly my mother, who, for all my adult years, had wrongly assumed that she had instilled the bed-making habit in her daughter. Woe to me, I had been living a lie.

That morning in April when I made my bed, I thoroughly repented of my twenty-five years of slothful behavior as Ms. RumpleSheets. I felt a quiet sense of accomplishment, standing in the doorway and admiring my feat of housekeeping bravado.

And then the craziest things started happening, there in that stream of morning light. I picked up a stray sock, and then a bobby pin, and then a small stack of unfolded clothes from the bedroom floor. (I didn't want the clutter messing with my serene sanctuary.) Then I went to the kitchen, cleared out the kitchen sink, loaded the dishwasher, and lit three candles. I pulled a metal pig from the corner of the kitchen and set him out, front and center, as a conversation piece. It took all of fifteen minutes.

My act of bed-making had set off a chain of small household tasks. And then I stood back and admired all of it, because *hi, I'm weird.*

I felt like a grown-up—a happy, legit grown-up with a made bed, a clean sink, one decluttered cupboard, and a pig on the counter. I felt like a woman who had miraculously pulled herself up from the energy-sucking Bermuda Triangle of Household Chaos.

And then I remembered that I still had my "crap stack"[6] of papers by the counter. The crap stack included graduation invitations, a weekly food journal, and a $92 speeding ticket that needed to be paid by the following Tuesday. (Work in progress, gentle readers. I'm a work in progress. Jesus came to deliver us from condemnation, but apparently not from the Lyon County sheriff's deputy who ticketed me.)

Months have passed, and I am still making my bed. Making one's bed—I now understand—is what millions of healthy, happy grown-ups around the world have been doing for centuries.

Plus, Gretchen Rubin tells us that it works to boost daily happiness. Rubin, author of *The Happiness Project*, writes, "Especially if you're feeling overwhelmed, picking one little task to improve your situation, and doing it regularly, can help you regain a sense of self-mastery."[7]

Even if the rest of my day is a disaster, I can still come home to a bed that I made with my own two hands. And that's no small thing at all in a world filled with headlines and daily headaches that make us decidedly unhappy.

(Sidebar conversation: Just as we have vowed to resist Happiness Shaming, we hereby swear not to take part in Bed-Making Shaming. Some of you are happily living in an unmade-bed environment. Grace and peace to you. Please read the following remarks in the happy, fun spirit in which they are intended.)

There's one more thing I want to tell you about making your bed. It's a WWJD thing. What would Jesus do? I thought you'd never ask.

Well, do you remember that little bit in Scripture where the linen cloth has been folded neatly in the tomb after the Resurrection?[8] You know what that means, right?

Jesus made his bed. I didn't cross-check that with the Greek or anything, but I'm pretty sure that's what it means. Moral of the story: if the Savior of the world could find the time to make his bed before his grand exit, then I can surely find the time to make mine.

"But don't you think the angels folded the cloth?" my husband asked me the other morning, attempting to destroy the only redeeming spiritual point of the last page of this chapter.

"No. That's not possible," I retorted, with the obvious guidance and wisdom of the Holy Spirit who lives and reigns within me. "Jesus would never have asked the angels to serve him by making his bed. He came not to be served, but to serve."

So there you have it, my Doer friends. Make your bed. It will change your life. It will make you happy. Plus, after all of that doing you've done all day, you'll need a peaceful place to rest your happy little head.

Digging Deeper •••••••••••••••

1. Whether or not you scored highly as a Doer, God has wired each of us to experience the blessing of work. What tasks bring you the most happiness? Do they bring you in-the-moment happiness, residual happiness, or both?

2. Jennifer addresses several red flags for Doers. Which, if any, do you most relate to?

3. Brother Lawrence, in the clatter of that kitchen, said he possessed this: "God in as great a tranquillity as if I were upon my knees at the blessed sacrament." How have you experienced the presence of God while doing everyday work?

4. What small tasks bring you daily happiness? How might you rearrange your day to make more room for the tasks that bring joy to your life?

CHAPTER 6

The Relater

❧

Of all the things that wisdom provides for living one's entire life in happiness,
the greatest by far is the possession of friendship.
EPICURUS

So you're a Relater, are you? (Even if you're not a Relater, read along. Chances are, you know several Relaters, and understanding their happiness styles will help you understand and love them better. Plus, we all can learn from each other!)

Welcome to the club of the inviters, the lovers, and the soul connectors. You are the ones who make room at the table, know the value of friendship, and fiercely protect the people you love.

As a Relater, you find supreme happiness in positive, meaningful relationships with others. You thrive in the company of friends and family. You understand deeply that one of the greatest determinants of happiness is having a sense of belonging. And when trouble inevitably comes in this life, you know how dangerous it is to be stuck by yourself.

You are a person of many layers, so not every characteristic of a Relater will fit you perfectly. But people tend to describe you as *loving* and *loyal*, and this makes you happy.

What Makes You Tick

You love: the warmth and security of close relationships. You guard yourself against loneliness. At your best, you allow yourself to be fully seen. You also make safe places for others to be seen—and loved just as they are.

If you had tomorrow afternoon free: you would most enjoy it by being with the people you love. To you, home isn't a place; it's people. You feel most at home when you're in the company of those you love.

You connect with God by: seeing how the earthly pleasure of belonging intersects with the heavenly joy of a relationship with Jesus. You don't see people as burdens to be managed, but as blessings to be loved through good times and bad.

You would be lost without: a tribe of very close friends. You're tickled pink when someone is sitting across the table from you. If life gets messy, you want to have names and numbers on speed dial. You need to know who will be there for you at 3 a.m., and you want them to count on you just the same.

People say you are: likeable and warm. You possess a keen ability to see people. You are tuned in to others' thoughts and feelings. You know the value of belonging. You love to be needed by people, and you will fight for the ones who are closest to you.

If you're at a dinner party: you couldn't care less what's on the menu. It's the company you keep that makes you smile.

Red Flags for Relaters

You're outside your happiness sweet spot when: you run to people before God. You can drain yourself emotionally by taking care of everyone else first. You might try to test other people's commitments to you. You distrust those who don't reciprocate in relationships. Ironically, we are all at our greatest risk of falling into sin or idolatry in the area where we are most wired to experience pleasure and happiness, so Relaters have to guard against putting people before God.

People who aren't afraid to speak truth to you would say: you rely too much on others for your happiness. You suffer from FOMO (fear of missing out).

You can feel unsettled when: you're alone, left out, or feeling unneeded by people who have relied on you in the past. You suffer greatly when relationships are broken or lost entirely.

You feel you've let God down when: you are in the midst of unresolved conflict or have experienced irreconcilable differences with someone who has been important in your life.

You feel shame when: people see you as unassertive even though you see yourself as diplomatic. People have accused you of avoiding conflict, but you see yourself as a peacekeeper. Sometimes you have secretly wished you weren't so sensitive and needy.

You shame others when: you think they aren't making enough time for their loved ones. It upsets you when people don't reciprocate by giving you the time and attention you have given to them. You are annoyed when people decline your invitations.

How to Be the Happiest You

You will be in your sweet spot when: you are consciously relating to others out of the love that Jesus first had for you. You are happiest when your relationships are Christ-centered. You can maximize your sweet spot by remembering that your first and most important relationship is the one you have with God. All other relationships flow from Jesus' friendship toward you.

You will stay in your sweet spot when: you guard against seeking the approval of people before the approval of God. You are happiest when you remember that your relational security comes from God first.

Avoid shaming yourself by: realizing we are all created differently. What brings you happiness might make your Doer friends hyperventilate. For instance, there's nothing wrong if, during a mission trip to Haiti, you would prefer hearing the stories of people in the village over painting fences and pounding nails.

Avoid shaming others by: realizing they were created for their own sweet spots too. Just as they have something to learn from you, you have something to learn from the Doers, Experiencers, Givers, and Thinkers. Like you, they were created in the image of God. On that mission trip, don't hassle your Doer friends for painting fences when they could have bonded with the people you met in the village.

You can love the Relaters in your life by: giving them what they want most of all—time with you and others. Allow yourself to be vulnerable and fully seen, which will give them permission to do the same. Let them know how much you appreciate the way they love and care for others—and how that reminds you of Jesus.

The Story of a Relater

In 2002, we moved back to my husband's family farm and built a house. I felt invisible in this new community.

I wanted friends, so I joined a Bible study, an exercise class, and a stay-at-home moms' group that met twice a month.

Yeah, everyone was super kind in this close-knit farming community. But guess how many of them wanted to be my actual friend? A big fat zero. It was like every potential friend slot was already taken.

I tried hard to fit in because that's what women do when things don't work out: We *try hard* like it's our job. Embarrassing fact: This is why I own every Pampered Chef gadget and every Tastefully Simple spice known to womankind. I wanted to make friends, so I was a home-party ninja. I hosted parties and invited anyone I knew—even casually—from church, the dentist's office, or the grocery store. I was so lonely that I found myself striking up friendly conversations with telemarketers.

Yes, I realize how desperate all of this sounds. I wanted someone to like me, so I practically killed myself trying to make it happen. My happy tank was empty during those early years on the farm, and I knew why. As much as I am a Doer, I am secondarily a Relater, according to the happiness style assessment. I need people.

We all need people.

We need friends with whom we can share our messiest selves. We need friends who will overindulge with us at Starbucks and who will help us find some shred of humor before getting a mammogram or a root canal. We all need someone who, during swimsuit season, will stand in solidarity beside us in adjoining changing rooms with those horrific fluorescent lights, flimsy curtains, and full-length mirrors. We need someone to tell us that we should never wear sensible shoes with skinny jeans—and to tell us when skinny jeans are about to go out of style.

We need someone to pray with us—and over us. And we want to do the same for others. We need someone to confide in *us*. We need a person to speak truth when we are a half step away from the dumbest decision of our lives. And we need someone to celebrate with us, rather than compete with us, over life's little triumphs.

But for years on that farm, I felt invisible to other women, and in some ways, invisible to God. Inside my loneliness, it felt safer to stop wishing than to believe that the impossible would ever happen.

Hoping for friends felt dangerous. What if true friendship never came? What if God had withheld relationships from me as punishment for not adequately appreciating the people he had put in my life before? I know—superbad theology. But when we believe that God wants something for his people and we don't get to have it, we assume it's our fault. We might believe that extended discomfort is proof we've done wrong or lacked faith in God.

If God wanted me in relationships with others, and I didn't

have them, where had I failed? I knew for sure that God had wired me for connection. Belonging is a fundamental, primal human need. It always has been. "It is not good for the man to be alone," God said in Genesis.[1] His words were directed toward marriage, but they also speak to one of our deepest inner needs: for friends and companions. God doesn't stop at wiring us *for* community. He *is* community. He is actually three persons—Father, Son, and Holy Spirit.

But without a close tribe of friends, I felt like God's favor was slipping away with my happiness. I felt soul sick. And it's no wonder why. We are always, always better together. Together is what makes us brave when life makes us scared. Together is what makes us strong when the world makes us feel weak. Healthy relationships boost happiness, no matter which of the five happiness styles we primarily identify with. All people need people. We belong to each other.

How much do relationships really matter when it comes to happiness? A lot, as it turns out. Relationships are like water—most of us can't survive without them. Research tells us that relationships are vital to our spiritual and physical health. One study showed that loneliness can actually be twice as unhealthy as obesity, if not deadly.[2]

Every year, Gallup conducts a poll to discover where the happiest people live on earth. Gallup compiles a "positive experience index score" for every country in the world. In 2014, the ten happiest countries on earth were all in Latin America. Every last one.[3] Politically and financially, this makes no sense. If happiness were in "things," many of these folks would be among the most dissatisfied on earth.

But the opposite is true.

Together is what
makes us brave
when life makes
us scared.

One observer suggested a plausible reason:

> Latin Americans have a list of priorities that are
> generally upside down compared to those of North
> America and other "modern" industrialized regions.
> Instead of making work, success, and wealth the most
> important things in life, Latin Americans typically
> have family and community firmly at the top of their
> priority list. . . . The time they spend with their family
> and friends is the most important time to them.[4]

Studies show that if you have five or more friends with whom to discuss important matters in your life, you're more likely to describe yourself as "very happy." But even one close friend can improve your life in profound ways.[5]

This isn't an extroverts-only club. Many introverts are also happiest when intimately connected. While introverts might prefer spending time with one or just a couple of friends rather than attending a big party, everyone is happier in community.

A Relater is a person who loves to invite family around the table for games and fondue. Or—get this—she might be the woman who hasn't gotten the nerve up to invite a friend to her table, but who is dying for an invitation to someone else's. Maybe that Relater is you.

How to Leave Your I-Land

The Christian poet John Donne famously wrote in 1624, "No man is an island."[6] But so many of us—even Relaters—are living unhappily as islands. Or as *I-lands*.

I lived on an I-land for four solid years. Sure, I had acquaintances. And yes, I had a good husband and wonderful daughters who made me feel loved and valued. I remember distinctly how badly Scott wanted to fix things for me—and how inadequate he felt when he knew how deeply I desired female friends. He once asked me, "Am I not enough?" He was enough as a husband, but he didn't make the best girlfriend. Something about the facial hair.

Research shows that, among women, one of the strongest predictors of well-being is healthy relationships with others. One study in particular underscores the importance of friendship in a profound way. A Stanford University researcher studied the survival rate of women with breast cancer. He found that women who had a strong, supportive circle of friends outlived, by many years, their counterparts who were socially isolated.[7]

Women need women.

I had been on my I-land for four years when I found a friend—long after I'd given up hope.

Actually, my friend found me. Her name was Michelle, and she found me at the end of a long table at her church during an ice-cream social we attended. Turns out, she had been praying for a friend too. The only difference was that she didn't stop praying. She never gave up. She knew that community was important and she was willing to fight for it.

Michelle is a Relater. And in the years that I've known her, she has taught me three important things about friendship:

1. Be the friend you want to have.
2. Go first.

3. If no one is inviting you to their table, invite someone
   to yours.

I had a place at Michelle's table. I had a place in her living-
room small-group study. And on her deck, with our feet propped
up on the wood railing. And in the pedicure chair next to hers.
And in the car on our way to Women of Faith weekends.

That was eleven years ago. We're still "dating," as we like to
say. We're still getting our toenails done, laughing at inappro-
priate times, and making fools of ourselves in public. We have
intimate knowledge of how accurate Ralph Waldo Emerson was
when he said, "It is one of the blessings of old friends that you
can afford to be stupid with them."

Michelle and I have loved each other through awesome days,
crappy days, and *meh* days. We understand each other's insides.
While we value our special bond, we look for ways to continue
making spaces at our own tables—because we both know how
awful it is to feel alone.

Even with a good friend like Michelle, I have gone through
painful seasons of loneliness due to changing life circumstances
and busyness. During those seasons, my happiness levels tanked.

A couple of years ago, I wrote my first book. While writing, I
learned how easy it is to gradually slide into isolation. My growing ministry demanded a busier speaking schedule, which made
me feel absent from my own life. The irony was not lost on me:
I'm primarily a Doer. I find supreme happiness in purposeful
activity. Doers maximize their happiness when they are doing
what they were created to do—and when they are doing it well.

But this Doer overdid. I stepped across the happiness thresh-
old and straight into lunacy. I had unwisely said *yes* to a lot of

really good things. But while focusing on all the good, I had lost sight of the very best.

The overdoing of my doing robbed me of the heart connection that my soul craved. Even as I poured out encouragement to others on conference stages, I was still the same Jennifer who needed someone to encourage her. I was still a human with real hurts and heart needs—not a machine. I was struggling with brokenness, and like most of you, I needed girlfriends to sit down with me in my mess and help me pick up the pieces. Like you, I needed someone who would ask me how I was doing and then stick around to hear the long answer.

I missed my friends. I missed my actual life.

So I entered what my friend Myquillyn calls "a season of no." When requests came to speak at conferences and retreats, I knew I had to decline. I needed to lasso some of my *do*ing in order to reunite with my *be*ing. And for me, *be*ing involved flesh-and-blood interaction with my husband and my sweet girls—but also with other grown-up women.

Shortly after entering my season of no, I attended a spiritual retreat with some girlfriends. For the first time in a long time, I didn't hold a microphone during the weekend. My friends and I had come to serve the retreat guests in a support role. Which means we prayed a lot. We washed dishes, served meals, swept floors, slept on bunk beds and giggled ridiculously loud, stayed up far too late, and nibbled on dark chocolate. I cried. I danced. I reconnected with old friends in meaningful ways.

That weekend was like food for my deep, underfed hunger. I learned that I wasn't the only one who felt relationally malnourished. Through tears, so many women I served with that weekend said they felt a hollowness on the inside. Each day, we servants gathered around a table for a time of prayer and devotions. One afternoon, our group leader read a devotional on friendship and loneliness. A few women began to cry. All around the table, women said they felt isolated, cut off, and unseen.

Loneliness enveloped these women in their beds at night and then first thing in the morning. It struck them in the silence of their marriages and cut through the noise of their toddler-commandeered houses. Loneliness sat beside them on the back pew, in the gymnasium bleachers, at the holiday parties. These women struggled with their marriages, decisions about jobs, infertility, and wayward children. But no one knew. These women felt like they had no one to call.

We are living in a time of strange relational paradox: We have more opportunities to network, but feel more disconnected than ever before. Our webs of connections grow ever wider . . . and ever shallower. You can have one thousand friends on Facebook and feel like the loneliest person on the planet.

We all want to belong. Even if you're not primarily a Relater, all people need people. It runs in the family. Our brother Jesus was a Relater too.

Jesus: The Ultimate Relater

Jesus did a lot of amazing things during his time on earth. One of those things was showing us what it means to be a true friend. Jesus shared tables with tax collectors and sinners. He didn't call his disciples *servants*, but instead called them *friends*. He had a tight band of about a dozen close friends, but he also had three friends who were especially close.[8]

When Jesus was transfigured on the mountain, his three closest friends—Peter, James, and John—were with him. Jesus "led them up a high mountain by themselves."[9] Later, those three men were the friends Jesus took with him during one of the most painful moments of his life—the night he agonized in the garden of Gethsemane. "'My soul is overwhelmed with sorrow to the point of death,' he told them. 'Stay here and keep watch.'"[10]

Like us, Jesus needed friends—when he was on the mountaintop and when he was in the valley.

Friendship is more than a good idea. It's a command from Christ: "This is my commandment, that you love one another as I have loved you. No one has greater love than this, to lay down one's life for one's friends. You are my friends if you do what I command you."[11]

When we make friends with people, we make friends with Jesus. And when we make friends with Jesus, we are happier, healthier people.

Sometimes we have to fight for our relationships. Because they are valued by God, they are targeted by the enemy. I have seen how the evil one works in the dark. Once upon a dreary time, the enemy wanted me to feel isolated and detached. He knew that if I didn't have friends or accountability partners around, I would grope in the dark, unable to adequately defend myself against his lies.

When I feel alone, my default response is to go deeper into my isolation and detach even more. But because I'm on to the enemy's tricks, I've taken a new approach. Instead, I tell someone I'm lonely. I let a friend know that I need a friend. I ask for someone to pray with me. I invite someone to lunch because I can't afford to wait for the invitation from someone else. I know that I have to do *something* because, if I don't, the enemy will sit in the empty chair next to me, whispering lies. In order to step into the light, I have to fight my way there by taking the first step out of the dark.

Boosting Your Happiness by Risking Vulnerability

Mature Relaters know that a shortcut to happiness is found in the scary land called *Vulnerability*. Vulnerability is intimidating because the more you expose your soul, the more you strip away your defenses. And without your defenses, how will you protect yourself?

When we slip out of our self-protective armor, we're saying, "Here is all of me. The parts where you can love me and the parts where you can hurt me." But when it comes to long-term happiness, Relaters know that the risk is worth the payoff.

I saw how this played out a few months ago when our younger daughter, Anna, hosted a sleepover for several of her friends. One of the mothers informed me that her daughter would be bringing along her "lovie" and was worried that the other girls might tease her for sleeping with a ragged blanket—the same blanket that she'd slept with for ten years straight. It had moved with her from her crib to her toddler bed to her "big girl" bed. The blanket had taken long car rides with her, and it had soothed her when she felt lonely or hurt or afraid of the dark.

When this girl was around the people who knew her and loved her best, she was never afraid to bring the lovie into the light. But as she grew older, she began to keep it hidden from everyone else. She couldn't quite put a finger on the reason why. Why did something she loved so much feel like it had to be hidden? Somehow, the blanket had become a bit of a secret. Admitting that she slept with a lovie made this girl feel vulnerable and maybe a bit ashamed.

As night came, I dimmed the lights in the family room, where Anna and her friends would sleep. All the girls snuggled under blankets for a late-night movie. I pushed play on the remote. But that girl? She wanted her blanket. I could see how she was fighting a quiet battle on her insides.

This battle was about the risk of vulnerability. If she's like most of us, Anna's friend was asking herself the most paralyzing question in the universe: *What will people think of me?*

She made her choice. I watched as she walked to the bedroom, unzipped her bag, and quietly pawed through her belongings to find the love-worn blanket. From my seat in the family room, I saw what happened next.

The girl walked back into the room with her blanket tucked under her arm. One of the girls saw what she had retrieved from the bag. The girl had been found out.

"What's that?" asked the friend, pointing a finger at the lovie.

I was so proud of that little girl, because here's what she did next: She lifted her chin, mustered her voice, and took the first step toward authentic relationship. She sat cross-legged on the couch and told her room of friends the truth. She told them how her mom's friend had made the blanket for her when she was a newborn, how it had traveled with her on a hundred car rides, how she once lost it at the park, and how it fell apart a few years ago so Grandma had to sew it back together. She showed everyone the long stitch mark, and it looked like a scar.

Everyone listened. No one laughed at her. No one judged. And then the most beautiful thing happened. One by one, each of the girls pushed back the covers, walked into the bedroom, and unzipped her own duffel bag. Out came the ragged blankets, a bear with a missing eye, a plush doll. *Every girl in the room was hiding a secret lovie in her bag.*

That was the Night of the Great Unzipping.

Each girl dragged her own lovie into the living room, and then they took turns telling their stories—about lovies loved, lovies lost, and lovies found again.

Everyone slept better that night. Because someone had the guts to go first.

Women in particular work hard to hold up defenses. We disguise what we think is wrong about us. We try hard to keep it all together because we are afraid of rejection. But those things that we believe are "wrong" about us actually make us approachable to every other woman who is struggling with her own set of wrongs. If we work hard to mask all of our messes, the woman on the other side of the room will never know that we are uniquely equipped to understand her pain. Our collective happiness is elevated when we all live as our realest selves. When we are vulnerable, we arrive at the place where we can rejoice with those who rejoice and weep with those who weep.[12] We can celebrate the good and help one another carry the bad. Just as God intended.

When we know who we are relationally with God, we are equipped to function relationally with others. It's when we know we're friends of God that we can truly be friends of people.

To be in community, you have to aggressively fight back

myths about other people and about yourself. Because the facts are these:

1. You are not the only one. Your inner crazy is universal.
2. You aren't in competition. There's more than enough goodness to go around.
3. You are seen.

Everyone goes through lonely seasons. On the days when you feel overlooked or alone, repeat over and over: "I am seen. I am known. I am loved. I am not invisible to God."

What a Friend We Have in Jesus

I've sung this hymn since I was a little girl—

What a friend we have in Jesus,
All our sins and griefs to bear![13]

Of every friendship I've ever had, none is more precious than the one I have with Jesus. I can think of no happier moments than those when I am intimately aware of Jesus' love for me. Are you looking to reap the gift of happiness today? Call on Jesus. And while you're at it, invite someone over. Risk vulnerability. Go first.

Make a plan with a friend and experience anticipatory happiness as you look forward to your time together. Wring out every ounce of delight when you're with her, so you can both experience in-the-moment happiness. Then remember fondly the good times you've had, even months later, to experience residual happiness.

According to psychology professor Sonja Lyubomirsky, a renowned expert on happiness, "If you begin today to improve and cultivate your relationships, you will reap the gift of positive emotions. In turn, the enhanced feelings of happiness will help you attract more and higher-quality relationships, which will make you even happier, and so on, in a continuous positive feedback loop."[14]

I believe that is true. With all my heart, I do.

But I also believe something else: When we are happy with our friends and family, we are drawn deeper into the heart of the one who loved us first.

The truth is, all relationships change. Some will grow richer and deeper with time. But some people we love will move away or turn away. Family members will die. All the relationships that make us so happy on earth will one day pass away, until we meet those people again in heaven.

There's an old poem that lists three types of friendships. According to that poem,

Some friends are with us for a reason.
Some friends are with us for a season.
But very few will walk beside us for a lifetime.

My friend Holley Gerth, an author and speaker, once shared that poem with me. It was a reminder that relationships change over the years. But that doesn't mean we've done something wrong. It doesn't mean we are being punished by God. Very few people will walk with us for a lifetime. If relationships change, Holley said, "it simply means God has a unique path for each of us. . . . And that's okay."

Even so, there's a 100 percent guarantee that there is someone who wants to walk alongside you for the rest of your life. That friend will never leave you. He will never abandon you. Nothing can separate you from his love—not even death.

His name is Jesus.

Digging Deeper ••••••••••••••••••

1. Whether or not you scored highly as a Relater, God has wired each of us to experience the blessing of community. What relationships in your life have brought you the most happiness—in the past and now?

2. Jennifer addresses several red flags for Relaters. Which, if any, do you most relate to?

3. "You can have one thousand friends on Facebook and feel like the loneliest woman on the planet," Jennifer writes. Can you relate to that phrase? Why or why not?

4. Jennifer retells a story about a little girl who revealed a "lovie" during "The Night of the Great Unzipping." How difficult is it for you to unzip your heart and share vulnerably with others?

CHAPTER 7

The Experiencer

❧

It is not how much we have, but how much we enjoy, that makes happiness.
CHARLES SPURGEON

So you're an Experiencer, are you? (Even if you're not an Experiencer, read along. Chances are, you know several Experiencers, and understanding their happiness styles will help you understand and love them better. Plus, we all can learn from each other!)

Welcome to the club of the beauty seekers, adventurers, and pay-attentioners. You have the enthusiasm of a child and a deep sense of wonder. You find supreme happiness by engaging in meaningful moments with a sense of adventure, curiosity, and whimsy—at home or on the road.

You don't look for happiness in a store. You look for it in moments.

You don't chase happy endings, because you're all about living the story.

You are a person of many layers, so not every characteristic of an Experiencer will fit you perfectly. But people tend to describe you as *enterprising* and *fun loving*, and that makes you happy.

What Makes You Tick

You love: the potential that every moment holds. You see beauty in places overlooked by others. With you, anything can be turned into an experience. You believe that experiences have far more happiness value than anything you can buy in a store.

If you had tomorrow afternoon free: you would enjoy it by being completely spontaneous. You might head off on an adventure, but you're not averse to staying close to home. The most important thing to you is that you live in the moment and wring as much happiness out of today as you can.

You connect with God by: seeing how the earthly pleasure of experiencing this world intersects with the heavenly joy of being grateful for all that God has given you. Each moment is to be enjoyed to its fullest because who knows if tomorrow will come?

You would be lost without: your sense of wonder. You value time off from the drudgery of routine, so vacations are important to you. But you try to be intentional about finding the good in everyday moments too.

People say you: love a good time. They call you spontaneous and idealistic. They admire how you stop to experience the beauty of a sunset, how you seem to appreciate the good in the world, and how you practice mindfulness when everyone else is too busy to notice.

If you're at a dinner party: you are in one of two places—planning some fun activity that includes the whole group, or standing on the back deck taking in the incredible lightning show overhead.

Red Flags for Experiencers

You're outside your happiness sweet spot when: you overindulge—thinking if one is good, ten is better. You may move on to the next fun thing at the expense of what needs to get done. Ironically, we are all at our greatest risk of falling into sin or idolatry in the area where we are most wired to experience pleasure and happiness, so Experiencers have to guard themselves against so-called "destination addiction," or believing happiness lies in the next best thing.

People who aren't afraid to speak truth to you would say: you are too easily distracted from the work you need to do. In stressful situations, you are prone toward escapism.

You can feel unsettled when: you aren't stimulated experientially. Despite your attempts at mindfulness, you sometimes struggle with boredom and feelings of sameness.

You feel you've let God down when: you've gotten so busy that you haven't stopped to smell the proverbial roses. If God went to the trouble of creating such a beautiful and fun world, it ought to be enjoyed.

You feel shame when: people pick up your slack because you haven't gotten things done. Sometimes you secretly wonder if you ought to be more disciplined.

You shame others when: you think they are too serious, too planned out, or too rigid. You may assume that you enjoy life more than others and may think that Experiencers have a superior happiness style.

How to Be the Happiest You

You will be in your sweet spot when: you are consciously connecting every gift this world has to offer with the God who happily created it all. You can maximize your sweet spot by deliberately inviting Jesus into your adventures and being grateful to God, knowing he is the source of what brings you such joy. Finding your highest happiness in God makes every happiness-inducing experience from him an even deeper pleasure.

You will stay in your sweet spot when: you guard against overindulging. You will need to consciously remind yourself that your joy is in Jesus, not in the experience itself, so that you don't miss the real source of your desire. Even on the boring days, remember that every day is a gift with great potential to be enjoyed.

Avoid shaming yourself by: realizing we are all created differently. What brings you happiness might make your Doer friends hyperventilate. For instance, there's nothing weird about you if you are the crazy aunt who takes all the nieces and nephews outside to make snow angels on Christmas Day—while the Doers stay in to dutifully wash the dishes.

Avoid shaming others by: realizing they were created for their own sweet spots too. Just as they have something to learn from you, you have something to learn from the Doers, Relaters, Givers, and Thinkers. Like you, they were created in the image of God. When a Doer in your life is still washing dishes as you make snow angels, remember that he or she is not a fun hater. He or she might actually enjoy working shoulder to shoulder with your mom at the sink.

You can love the Experiencers in your life by: giving them what they want most of all—space and time to experience all this world has to offer. For birthdays, consider planning an event that celebrates your Experiencer loved ones rather than buying them gifts at the store. Let them know how much you appreciate the way they engage with the world—and how they seem grateful for the gifts that God has given them.

The Story of a Reluctant Experiencer

Confession: I am adventure averse.

Remember, I'm a type-A, rule-following woman who loves lists, straight lines, and carefully crafted plans. I find happiness in a well-organized pantry and a weeded garden. I use the sidewalk instead of cutting through the grass. If I unleash my inner wild girl and break the rules, there's a 92 percent chance I'll get caught.

I am a Doer. When I took my happiness style assessment, Experiencer came in dead last. I realize how unfun this makes me sound. Hang with me. Remember our rule about happiness shaming: there is no one superior sweet spot of happiness.

I could learn something about happiness from the people in my life who are Experiencers. Including my own children.

Because of my proclivity toward structure, I am one of those good-intentioned mothers who used to make a list at the start of every summer. On the list: a multitude of wholesome and educational activities I'd love to do with the girls throughout the summer months.

I would buy glossy math workbooks in May, hoping that the extra work would help the children retain what they learned the previous school year—and maybe have a jump on the new season of learning. I would pledge to do flash cards, visit every museum in a one-hundred-mile radius, study star charts, participate faithfully in the library's book club, and take leisurely nature walks to give my daughters a sense of appreciation for horticulture and geology.

One year I announced my plans to the girls on the first day of our summer break. Lydia and Anna were eating a well-balanced breakfast of scrambled eggs, whole-wheat toast, yogurt, and strawberries. I fanned out their school pencils in front of my face, resharpened and ready.

"Just a little worksheet! Nothing too hard, I promise. Just one a day." My eyes widened to saucers and reflected every exclamation point that I felt on the inside. "It will be fun!"

Both of my girls stared blankly at me as they slowly chewed their toast. Then they skittered to a far corner of the house to plot out a summer with more sunscreen and ice cream. For whatever reason, their plans eclipsed mine that year.

I don't know how it happened exactly, but we accomplished very little on that list of mine. We visited exactly one museum. If the breakfasts were well balanced, the credit went to the vitamin fortification of boxed cereal. Our geology lessons amounted to a rock collection I discovered after I heard something sounding like an avalanche coming from the clothes dryer. And that arsenal of workbooks? Maybe the girls hid them. I watched with resignation as my good intentions were torched in the midsummer heat.

The girls had clearly commandeered the reins of summer. Looking back on it now, I'm so grateful. Here's why: I got a taste of what it is to find happiness as an Experiencer, and I learned what it means to love someone well when her happiness style differs from my own.

Like many children, our daughters have strong Experiencer tendencies. Their play *is* their work. And on an August afternoon, their sweet spots of happiness landed our family of four at the mouth of a water-park ride in Wisconsin called the Howlin' Tornado.

You must know this: I'm allergic to water parks. Well, not technically allergic. But water parks are just so . . . squishy. And wet. And overrun with feral children.

If I have to go to a water park, you'll find me in a reclined chair with a book—or rocking back and forth in a corner with a crazed look in my eye. But the girls would have none of that. They led me and their dad up approximately fifty-two flights of stairs to ride the Howlin' Tornado. Together we carried a mammoth inflatable tube on our backs.

When we got there, it was clear to me: We were about to enter into a swirling vortex of terror. Fragile human beings were being thrown by the force of the water into the "thrill" ride— *thrill* being a term one should use loosely.

Then it was our turn. Our mammoth inflatable suddenly felt like a toddler-size floaty toy. I made a mad grab for one of the tube's handles. And off we went, into the tornado. The ride must get its "howlin'" moniker from the *howling* mothers who plummet into its depths for the love of their children, so that her offspring might one day "rise and call her blessed."

I howled. The girls whooped. My husband cackled hysterically.

And then? We did it again. And again, to defy all common sense and the advancing hand of death.

On our tenth trip down, I saw Anna whispering to her older sister. I asked her what they were scheming. "Well," Anna said hesitantly, "I'm not sure I should tell you this, but . . . um . . . Dad told us to watch your face during the ride because it's the funniest thing ever."

Yeah, I was terrified. But you know what else? For thirty minutes of my life, I was completely caught up in an unforgettable moment with my family. We gave our girls a gift: the opportunity to experience their own sweet spots of happiness, unhindered.

During that trip, I didn't once think about the kind of stuff that keeps me up at night or the deadlines I was facing back home. I didn't think about bills, hurt feelings, or squishy water-park chairs. That day was one of my favorite summer memories of the year. I was consumed by happiness.

Sometimes happiness is an inner peace. Sometimes it's a feeling of satisfaction. But sometimes it's a wild ride that makes your soul erupt like a boxful of fireworks. Sometimes the wildest ride of happiness is one that you never dreamed of taking in the first place.

Perhaps we could let children lead us, for they hold a key to unlock uninhibited happiness. And perhaps to unlock the child that is living right inside each of us.

If you are an Experiencer, chances are that you are one of the "fun friends" who wouldn't think twice about eating ice cream for breakfast. You are the mountain hikers, the skydivers, the white-water rafters, and the ones daring enough to sleep under the stars without worrying about the creepy-crawlies. You are the first ones on the dance floor and the last ones to leave the party.

But Experiencers aren't merely thrill seekers or adrenaline junkies. Experiencers encounter God's delight in the quiet, hallowed places too.

One of my favorite Experiencer stories comes from Ann Voskamp's *One Thousand Gifts*. The scene unfolds when her husband, a farmer, peeks his head in the door of the house and motions her to follow him. She's making supper, busy with the task of feeding six children. But he insists because he knows her. He knows how God speaks to his wife in the wild places, in the out-of-doors, in the *experience* of coming face-to-face with God's glory in Creation.

The farmer himself is a picture of happiness too. In the story Ann tells us, her husband is part man, part child.

He's grinning silly, man-boy with a secret he can hardly contain.

He leads me the impossible distance of a whole two steps to the windowsill. I'm transfixed. Wonder gapes the mouth open. . . .

His whisper brushes the curl of my ear, "When I saw it, I knew you'd want it too."[1]

What did he want her to see? The moon, a flame burning up the sky. Ann grabbed her camera and ran for the fields. "I am gone, out the back door, across the back lawn, apron still on. I take flight. I feel foolish . . . but I feel four again."[2]

Ann chases the moon. A palpable happiness transports her

straight into the heart of God, all of her tasks momentarily forgotten. She is smitten, lost in holy love.

"I laugh. I am still a child,"[3] Ann writes.

Yes, the Experiencers are the skydivers and the globe-trotters and the cliff divers. But they are also the moon chasers, the campfire makers, and the daisy pickers. They may be twenty-eight or fifty-two or eighty-nine, but on the inside, they're forever four.

And with a child's eyes, the Experiencers help us see straight into the heart of Jesus.

The Holy Happiness of the Experiencer

Ann was chasing the moon. But she was mostly chasing God. And in following both God and the moon that he created, she found utter joy.

Augustine knew that both God and happiness are intertwined like that. "Following after God is the desire of happiness; to reach God is happiness itself," he wrote.[4] Experiencers understand this: The best experiences aren't escapes from life, but encounters with Christ.

My friend Michelle scores highly as an Experiencer. She plans spontaneous trips to the latest Chris Tomlin concert or the movies. She is the friend who organizes the last-minute dinner party and doesn't worry if the pizza gets burned. She calls it "making a memory."

"Even if it doesn't go as we planned," Michelle says, "we were still together. We were making a memory, and that's what it's all about." She understands that shared experiences connect us to each other and to God. Experiences are important because they become a part of who we are. They become a part of the stories we tell one another.

All of us are the sum of our moments lived.

Researchers suggest that Michelle's approach toward living can unlock huge stores of happiness for the rest of us. People of all happiness types can benefit from planned experiences—such as vacations. The happiness of a vacationer begins well before the moment your toes touch the beach. Happiness begins the day you decide to go.

Experiencers feel great amounts of anticipatory happiness—the kind of joy that springs up inside of you when you are looking forward to a happy time. Experiencers enjoy the moment, but they get an extra happiness boost when they visualize what's to come. Anticipatory happiness is the happiness that comes when you tell your best friend you're going to Cancún, when you make an iTunes playlist for your hike, or when you explore the city map for the best place to have a family picnic.

Experiencers also experience residual happiness—the kind of joy that springs up after you recall the experiences you've had, even months or years later. Even the most imperfect experiences have the potential for residual happiness. We've all had experiences that we planned and anticipated, only to see them flop despite our best intentions—the beach vacation that was ruined by rain, the flight delays, the family fight, the flu bug that infected everyone on Christmas morning, the birthday cake that fell on the floor. Those messy experiences become funny stories to tell when the family reflects on them years later. Like Michelle says, you've made a memory.

That's why many researchers will tell you that if given the choice, you'll almost always be happier if you buy an experience—

like tickets to the symphony—instead of purchasing a pair of designer jeans.[5]

"People will say, well, you know, we stayed in [during the rainy beach vacation] and we played board games, and it was a great family bonding experience," says researcher Amit Kumar. Negative experiences, in other words, can be seen positively later on.

"That's harder to do with material purchases," Kumar says. "When my Macbook has the colorful pinwheel show up . . . I can't say, well, at least my computer is malfunctioning!"[6]

Kumar's words make sense to the Experiencer inside of me, begging to bust loose.

Happiness isn't about what we can hold in our hands. It's about what we hold in our hearts.

Jesus: The Ultimate Experiencer

We could easily characterize Jesus as a Thinker and certainly as a Giver. But an Experiencer?

Oh . . . yeah.

Picture the scene with me. There's a boat on a lake, and the fishermen sitting inside it aren't catching a thing.

Meet your fishermen: Simon Peter, Thomas, Nathanael, the sons of Zebedee, and two other disciples. I don't know what kinds of conversations they had on that boat, but something tells me there was a lot of animated reminiscing about the events of the previous days. Jesus had died, been resurrected, and appeared to the disciples behind locked doors. If anyone had reason to be happy, these guys did. But even the happiest people get hungry. So they had gone out to fish.

Happiness isn't about what we can hold in our hands. It's about what we hold in our hearts.

Early in the morning, a man from the shore called out to them, "Friends, haven't you any fish?"

They answered back flatly, "No."

The man told them to throw their net on the right side of the boat. When they did, the catch was so large they weren't able to haul in the net. They didn't realize just yet that the man on the shore was Jesus.

I picture Jesus in this scene with a boyish grin. I have to laugh at his sense of humor here. He was about to give them an incredible, exhilarating experience—an unforgettable moment they would remember for the rest of their lives, a moment that would point straight to God himself.

Just then John said to Peter, "It is the Lord!"

Upon hearing this, Peter jumped into the water and swam for shore, where Jesus had built a fire, cooked fish, and brought bread.

"Come and have breakfast," Jesus said to Peter and the other disciples. Imagine the happiness around the fire.

Afterward, Jesus commissioned Peter. And in a beautiful scene, Jesus gave Peter an opportunity to repent from his past denials of Christ.[7] Jesus could have done this same thing in the coldness of a confessional booth. He could have preached the same lessons from the shore. He could have taught from a hillside. But he did something far more beautiful. He made breakfast. He created an experience on the beach.

Throughout the Gospels, we see Jesus as a divine person who enjoys the gifts of the created world. He attended weddings, sat down with children, enjoyed dinners with friends. In feats that would put all skydivers and cliff climbers to shame, he walked on water, calmed the wildest storms, and brought dead people to life. Jesus was the ultimate Experiencer.

I wonder how many of Jesus' experiences remain untold. John ends his Gospel with these words: "Jesus did many other things as well. If every one of them were written down, I suppose that even the whole world would not have room for the books that would be written."[8]

Jesus' experiences were never an end unto themselves. Every experience, every dinner, every hillside gathering, and every death-to-life miracle pointed directly at the source: God, the Giver of all happiness.

Some of us are skeptical of experiential happiness because we view the created world suspiciously. True enough, many pursuits of happiness lead straight to sin. But God didn't create this world to distract us from him; he created it as a means to love and enjoy him.

The "world" is not the enemy. The world is God's handiwork. David Naugle writes, "The genius of the Christian faith . . . is that it does not call upon us to eliminate our love for things on earth out of our love for God in heaven. It's not either God or the world, but both God and the world in a proper relationship."[9]

Because of Christ, our experiences are imbued with deeper meaning—every sighting of the moon, every breakfast on the shore, every fishing trip with your friends. When you fall more in love with God, you gain an even greater appreciation for the common and uncommon experiences of your life: eating a leisurely breakfast at the kitchen table, watching Netflix with your fluffy puppy warming your feet, hitting the high notes on the bridge of a song, swinging in a hammock, or watching the northward flight of geese.

Finding your highest happiness in God makes every happiness-inducing experience from him an even deeper pleasure. C. S. Lewis knew it when he wrote these words:

> It would seem that Our Lord finds our desires not too strong, but too weak. We are half-hearted creatures, fooling about with drink and sex and ambition when infinite joy is offered us, like an ignorant child who wants to go on making mud pies in a slum because he cannot imagine what is meant by the offer of a holiday at the sea. We are far too easily pleased.[10]

John Piper, author of *Desiring God*, helps us further understand what Lewis meant: "Our mistake lies not in the intensity of our desire for happiness, but in the weakness of it."[11]

Yes, of course, there remains danger in the experiences of the world. There remains the potential to pervert experiences that bring us happiness. That's the tricky thing about idols. Just as I, a Doer, have to guard against workaholism, an Experiencer has to guard against worshipping the gifts instead of the Giver.

One British psychologist warns Experiencers and all of us of "destination addiction."[12] Destination addicts rush through as many experiences as possible. They visit eight European cities in a week. They hike through the forest but miss all the trees.

Several years ago, my husband and I went to Maui with his family. While we were there, we drove the Road to Hana. The daylong road trip takes travelers along the rugged coastline of Maui.

We journeyed along the winding, wiggling worm of this legendary road. We wound our way past jaw-dropping beauty: verdant rain forests, slack-key guitarists, plunging pools, dramatic seascapes, veils of mists, and waterfalls.

All the tourist brochures will tell you that the journey is called *the Road* to Hana. No one calls the trip *Hana*. The road, it seems, is the attraction. It has a purpose greater than moving travelers from one place to another; the Road itself carries its own magic.

The Road was beautiful and lush, but it was also fraught with pesky bugs, hairpin turns, and carsickness caused by a slithering course with hundreds of curves and bumps.

The Road to Hana holds a lesson for us. It is this: Happiness isn't a destination. It's a journey. And sometimes the journey is hard. Sometimes the journey looks intimidating and downright impossible.

But Jesus is saying to us: *Trust me. I have something to show you. Experience this one life I have given you. It is all a gift.*

For those of us in Christ, Jesus is both Hana and the road there. He is both the destination and the way.

Mandatory Fun

Perhaps we need to chase more moons, eat more bacon,[13] take more bumpy roads and hairpin curves, and trust that we'll find beauty along the way.

Good heavens, I know that I don't always do that. I know how hyperfocused and dead serious I can be. Watch me some days at my desk—all furrowed brow with a dash of panic and a side of manic. Watch my fingers fly freakishly fast, and watch my intensity build as the end of my workday draws nigh.

On those days, I seriously need to cut my own joy-deprived soul some slack. On those days, behold: there sits my soul, curled up in a ball near my clavicle, all shriveled and thirsty for humor. *Poor thing.* We all need to throw back our heads and go into a complete giggle fit over the goodness of God.

My editor Sarah, also a Doer, has a solution for those of us prone to overworking ourselves. She blocks out a day every now and then for what she calls "mandatory fun."

"You *will* sit in the sunshine next to that rosebush for *fifteen minutes* and you *will* enjoy it," Sarah explains. "Then after the time is up, we *are* going to eat *ice cream*. And we'll *like* it!"

Without experiences, I may miss the miracle of ordinary moments outside of my office. I may forget that some days, the *interruptions* are my work.

It went down like that one day when my friend Sandy called. I let the phone ring four times before answering because you never know what you might agree to when Sandy calls. But I answered, and sure enough, she had an idea: *Could we go to the nursing home to play bingo?*

I inhaled one long stream of air. I scrunched my nose and closed my eyes tight, like if I tightened up my face enough, I might be able to wring my brain like a dishrag for some good excuse that would drip out of my head. *I mean, really*—how could I cram another thing into the little calendar box assigned for the day? That box was already pencil-scratched clear full.

Sandy interrupted the uncomfortable quiet space between us. "Jennifer, it's okay, truly. You don't have to . . ."

"I'm so sorry . . . ," I muttered, and the phone went back on the cradle.

I threw my head back, staring at the ceiling for a while. Then

I looked back down at the calendar boxes, always filling—page after calendar page. I drummed at a calendar square with the eraser end of my pencil. I wondered: *How many miracles have I missed between the thin lines of all those neatly penciled boxes?*

I stared up at the ceiling again. And I swear to you: It was like God was looking down at me with his arms crossed over his burly chest, his holy head tilted, and one eyebrow raised. I can't say for sure, but he might have been smirking.

"Fine." I said it out loud.

I lifted the phone off the cradle. Maybe I could go after all, I told Sandy.

"Be there at 2 p.m.," Sandy said.

At the nursing home, the room was dappled in sunlight, which reflected off wheelchair chrome and a Mylar "Happy Birthday" balloon. One of the women was celebrating her ninety-sixth year on earth. Tables were set with fake daffodils in slender white vases. I grabbed a bingo card and found a seat by a sweet lady we'll call Margaret.

Sandy was already there, calling bingo numbers into the microphone. "B-16. Does anyone have B-16?" Sandy asked.

A wide grin spread across Margaret's face. She bellowed: "Sweet sixteen and never been kissed!" Her shoulders shook as she laughed.

"B-18," Sandy called out. "B-18. Anybody remember when you were eighteen?"

Margaret's age-spotted hand shot into the air. "I do!" she shouted from her wheelchair. "I remember!"

Sandy asked into the microphone, "What would you do if you were eighteen again, Margaret?"

Margaret's eyes widened. She didn't hesitate. "I'd pick more daisies," she said. "And I'd dance barefoot in the rain and I'd fish with a worm." Margaret tossed her head back with laughter, looking up at the ceiling. Just at the ceiling, like she could see God up there. Like he was laughing with her.

And there were no calendar boxes anymore, not for Margaret.

I watched her with my chin resting in my hands.

I want to be a dancer. I want to be a daisy picker. I want to laugh more, laugh fuller. I want to put a worm on the hook of life, go fishing, and expect Jesus to show up on the beach.

What if—for the rest of my life—I made a little more time to live each day like the Experiencers do? What if, every once in a while, I added some mandatory fun to my week? What if I awoke to wonder and remembered that days are mere blips and that I could live more poetry in my own skin if I colored outside the lines?

Often, happiness unfolds inside my office. I'm grateful for that. But sometimes it happens outside of it.

What if I took one giant leap outside my safe boxes, made a holy mess of my to-do list, and then laughed with friends over the fun we had?

In the nursing home, I reached across the table and grabbed Margaret's hands. I told her how someday we'd dance together. She looked at me, puzzled, and then asked, "What are you waiting for?"

And she lifted our hands—just our hands, high to the ceiling—and she waltzed them through the air. And I swear, with just our hands, we danced. And we danced.

Digging Deeper •••••••••••••••••

1. Whether or not you scored highly as an Experiencer, God has wired each of us to approach the world with a sense of wonder. What is the last thing you saw/tasted/heard/experienced that made you pause to marvel at the creativity of God?

2. Jennifer addresses several red flags for Experiencers. Which, if any, do you most relate to?

3. Research tells us that if given the choice, we'll be happier if we buy an experience instead of an item at the store. Would you agree? Why or why not?

4. John Piper wrote, "Our mistake lies not in the intensity of our desire for happiness, but in the weakness of it." Reflect for a moment on that quote. Do you agree or disagree? Why?

CHAPTER 8

The Giver

No one has a right to consume happiness without producing it.

HELEN KELLER

So you're a Giver, are you? (Even if you're not a Giver, read along. Chances are, you know several Givers, and understanding their happiness styles will help you understand and love them better. Plus, we all can learn from each other!)

Welcome to the club of the helpers, the sharers, and the light bearers. You believe this: The best way to find happiness is to create happiness for someone else.

As a Giver, you find supreme happiness by seeking ways to bring delight to others. You believe that a shared happiness is a double happiness. You are the somebody who makes everyone else feel like a somebody.

You are a person of many layers, so not every characteristic of a Giver will fit you perfectly. But people tend to describe you as *thoughtful* and *selfless*, and that makes you happy.

What Makes You Tick

You love: to help others. You are tuned in to others' needs, and you gladly step in to help. You are supportive of others with your time, your words, your money, and your prayers.

If you had tomorrow afternoon free: you would most enjoy the day by doing whatever your family or friends preferred to do. You are happy when they are happy. You are also the kind of person who would enjoy taking the afternoon to volunteer at church or in your community.

You connect with God by: seeing how the earthly pleasure of giving intersects with the heavenly joy of God, who gives all gifts and inspires your giving. You know that God loves a cheerful giver, and when you are at your best, his pleasure is your driving motivation.

You would be lost without: your ability to help others. Knowing that you've succeeded in bringing happiness to another human soul boosts your happiness.

People say you are: reliable, helpful, and generous. You are willing to work behind the scenes without receiving credit. If someone needs help, you come to that person's mind immediately. You are the kind of person who brings your own sunshine, no matter how cloudy the sky.

If you're at a dinner party: you may well have planned the gathering. You enjoy the role of hostess—filling cups, serving snacks, and making sure everyone is comfortable.

Red Flags for Givers

You're outside your happiness sweet spot when: you forget about yourself. You can become physically and emotionally drained from taking care of others. You rarely ask for what you need. You take care of yourself last and may feel like your needs don't matter as much as someone else's. At your worst, you hide your needs and deny others the opportunity to give to you. At times, you see people as projects. Ironically, we are all at our greatest risk of falling into sin or idolatry in the area where we are most wired to experience pleasure and happiness, so Givers run the risk of becoming people pleasers.

People who aren't afraid to speak truth to you would say: you have a hard time saying no. You tend to minimize your own needs and the importance of self-care. Those closest to you worry that you may be taken advantage of without realizing it. They get frustrated because you don't reveal your true self and true needs.

You can feel unsettled when: your attempts to help others fail to produce the happiness in them that you had hoped for. You are deflated when the people who have needed you no longer need your help. It makes you nervous when people ask what you need.

You feel you've let God down when: you have to say no to someone who has asked you to serve or help out.

You feel shame when: people second-guess your motives. Sometimes you secretly wish that the opinions of others didn't matter so much to you, and you fear that you come off as an overaccommodating people pleaser and a "fixer."

You shame others when: they don't see the great need in the world that you see. You may develop a feeling of superiority or a sense of martyrdom when you are giving more than others. You may think that your happiness style is superior to others' because of Jesus' emphasis on giving and generosity.

How to Be the Happiest You

You will be in your sweet spot when: you are consciously giving to others out of the love that Jesus first had for you. You will be happiest and find life most meaningful when you give, not out of compulsion, but out of pure-heartedness, without expecting anything—such as someone's applause—in return.

You will stay in your sweet spot when: you don't attach strings to your giving. Your happiness levels will rise when you remember to value your own needs and let other Givers enjoy the grace of giving to you—just as you have enjoyed giving. It will be important for you to watch for signs of burnout, so that you don't begin to resent the good work that God has called you to do.

Avoid shaming yourself by: realizing we are all created differently. What brings you happiness might make your Experiencer and Relater friends wonder if you've gone mad. For instance, there's nothing wrong with you if you would prefer to work at the soup kitchen on a Saturday night instead of going to the concert with your besties.

Avoid shaming others by: realizing they were created for their own sweet spots too. Just as they have something to learn from you, you have something to learn from the Doers, Relaters,

Experiencers, and Thinkers. Like you, they were created in the image of God. When your friends are headed to the concert, don't inadvertently guilt them by making them think they ought to serve the homeless with you.

You can love the Givers in your life by: offering them what they want most of all—an opportunity to help you and see that your needs are met. Realize that when they are in their sweet spots, they are giving out of a deep love for you and for Jesus, and ultimately they have your happiness in mind.

The Story of a Giver

One night, a man showed up unexpectedly on our front doorstep while fat snowflakes fluttered down like feathers from heaven, glistening in the moonlight. My husband, Scott, opened the door. The man stepped in, stamping his snowy feet on the rug. Winter exhaled a frosty cloud into our house.

My hands were wrist-deep in dishwater, so I couldn't see the man at our door. But his voice was familiar, and it hurtled into the kitchen with urgency.

"I need to give this to Jennifer," he told my husband.

I felt panicky on the inside. *Is everything okay?* I dried my hands on a dish towel, stepped around the corner, and moved fast toward the door. The man unfolded a yellow slip of paper and handed it to me.

On the paper was a long list of names. He pointed with a gloved finger. My name was among them.

God had laid it on his heart to ask twenty-eight people in our little community to hand-deliver Applebee's gift cards to twenty-eight different people. He paid for all the gift cards, but he wanted them to be delivered anonymously. He asked God's help in finding Christmas helpers to deliver the gift cards on his behalf.

He handed me one of the gift cards, and then he read detailed instructions he had written on that same yellow paper. He said I needed to take that gift card to the college where I taught journalism at the time. Still reading, he added, "You're supposed to give this to someone and tell the person, 'God cares for you, and so do I.'"

He looked up from his paper, and I tripped over my words when I tried to reply. "I'm supposed to . . . um . . . *what*? Who do I give it to?"

He shook his head and answered, "I don't know who. I just know that you're supposed to give it to someone at the college."

"I will do that," I answered, standing up a little straighter and surer. And then, just like that, a name popped into my head, like a little deposit from the Holy Spirit. "I know who the person is."

He nodded a knowing nod. The Holy Spirit had whispered names to him too—including mine. That was why he had come to our door.

This man knew that it was more blessed to give than to receive, but he didn't want those who received his gift to know who the giver was. So he was stopping at the doorsteps of twenty-eight people on a blustery December night to recruit his army of Christmas helpers.

I asked if I could look at his paper again. At the top were dollar amounts, scratched out.

$550

~~$575~~

~~$600~~

~~$675~~

And then finally: $700.

God kept giving him names, he said, so the number he would need to spend on gift cards grew and grew and grew.

"I finally put my hands over my ears like this," the man said, laughing and demonstrating. "And I went: 'La-la-la-la-la! I'm not listening anymore, or I'm going to go broke, God!'"

This was not a rich man. This was a regular middle-class Iowa guy, a husband and dad who worked at a factory and liked watching ESPN. He drove a used car. He wore secondhand jeans and Walmart shirts.

He wouldn't let me tell you his name.

"Maybe we could have gotten a new TV with the money. But this is what I'm supposed to do," he said, shrugging. "It's a gift from God. You can't tell anyone who did it because this is from God—not me."

He knew it was from God, because at 11 a.m. on a Tuesday, God put name . . . after name . . . after name on his heart. And he transcribed. He wrote names on that yellow slip of paper.

And now he needed elves to spread Jesus' love at Christmas. Each person on his list would receive a twenty-five-dollar gift card to Applebee's. Each one had been instructed to give the gift to someone else.

A neighbor boy down the road was supposed to give a card to someone at the elementary school. A man who sells Doritos and Snickers to stock the shelves of area convenience stores had a card to give. So did a stay-at-home mom, a teenage girl, a schoolteacher, a coach, a farmer, a nurse, a grandpa, and a local business owner. I was supposed to give mine to someone at the college.

I read down the list and just shook my head and began to cry. Remembering it now, in the middle of my own Happiness Dare, brings fresh tears to my eyes. I remember seeing firsthand how this man's obedient act of giving—springing from an inner happiness in Jesus—had the potential to exponentially increase happiness for a multitude of others. And we—this little army of deliverers—got to take part in this wild act of giving, this extravagant generosity of an anonymous man.

That man, like most of us, has had some hard knocks in life. My husband and I have known him for years, and we have had a front-row seat to some of his hurts. We also saw what happened to him the year Jesus grabbed hold of his heart. That year, he still recalls, "I traded all the gray T-shirts in my dresser drawers for colorful ones because God brought color to my life."

I wish you could see how he lit up with joy that night in December, like a candle flickering atop a Christmas cake. It's true what they say about candles—they lose nothing by lighting another candle. They only add to the light, in a world that feels so dark.

Sometimes the darkest dark feels like a shadow inside the depths of us, especially during those seasons when we feel we've lost our way. We've all been there—groping around our dark inner rooms, looking for a window or a cracked door so we can find the light again.

The fastest way out of your darkest dark is to turn on the light for someone else, to give a bit of your own light. Giving away your own light will never, ever subtract from your supply—even if you feel like you've only got a sliver of flame to give. Instead, it will multiply the light, like candles around a sanctuary on Christmas Eve.

The Givers, like the man at our front door, teach us this: The best way to find happiness is to create happiness for someone else.

The Givers of our world are the candles of the earth. They know that shared light is a double light. When you share your happiness with someone, it isn't a happiness divided. It's happiness multiplied.

The Givers show up before you even thought to ask. They are the ones who pay for a whole line of coffees at Starbucks but quietly slip away before anyone gives them credit. They are the ones who will pick up your dry cleaning, organize the church's food drive, and stop by with chicken noodle soup on your terrible, horrible, no good, very bad days.

Givers are the women from my Mothers of Preschoolers group who showed up with a stack of tinfoil-covered casserole dishes after I fell down the stairs and injured my ankle. They are the friends who showed up when Scott's dad died, offering to clean the house and take care of the kids while we handled funeral arrangements. They are the feet washers and the kindness givers, the Kleenex bringers and the joy donors when the rest of us are running on empty. They bring good words and cupcakes, hot tea and hope.

Giving is countercultural because it puts us second. But Givers prove to the rest of us how the prevailing me-first attitudes about happiness are completely off the mark. When we are dwelling in the sweet spot of happy giving, we put others first.

Do you want to exponentially boost your happiness today? Give. Give with a cheerful heart. Give with your pocketbook or your time, your compassion or your prayers. It doesn't matter how you give. But if you do, God says you will have a 100 percent guaranteed return of happiness, depositing goodness into your own life: "If you give yourself to the hungry and satisfy the desire of the afflicted, then your light *will* rise in darkness and your gloom *will* become like midday."[1]

Not might. Not maybe. "Your light will rise." "Your gloom will become like midday."

You don't have to be a missionary to be a Giver. You don't have to be a Bill Gates either.

You might be a mom.

The Giving Heart of a Mother

Many mothers and grandmothers I know are Givers. And no, you don't have to be a mom to be exceptional at giving. Many of my dearest friends have never given birth to children and are some of the most selfless Givers I know. (And, sadly, I know of mothers who weren't Givers at all, who never gave to their children what was required.)

But I would be remiss if I didn't highlight the heart of mothers in a chapter about giving.

So many mamas find their sweet spots of happiness by serving their favorite people on earth—their families. Mamas would move heaven and earth and Mount Kilimanjaro-ish piles of laundry to bring happiness to their homes. Their hands smell like Johnson & Johnson lavender lotion or Vicks VapoRub. Their aprons are caked with cookie dough. Mama Givers slip love notes into their kids' lunch boxes. They stitch prayers into the knitted caps they make for their grandbabies.

Givers are the reason many women of childbearing age have what's commonly known as "bleacher butt." Those mamas give with their whole selves, including their backsides.

When I was growing up, my mom was a Doer, but she combined her doing beautifully with acts of service that made her one of the kindest, goofiest Givers I've ever known.

I seriously never minded being sick as a kid. It meant that my mom's theatrics were about to go on parade. She would come dancing into the room, popping her head through the doorway while wearing a crazy Halloween mask or singing a silly song in exaggerated vibrato. It's not that Mom didn't love me on my healthy days. But the sick days? Those were the best because she stroked my cheeks and tucked stray strands of hair behind my ears.

I have to believe that her small acts of giving increased her own happiness. Now that I'm a mother, I know how that works. When my girls are sick, I can assuage my own panicky feelings when I cuddle next to them in their beds, holding a washcloth to their foreheads and giving them every bit of my attention.

But sometimes the happiness is hard to find, no matter how much we try to give.

Last year, our daughter Anna grew increasingly ill. She had intense pain in her belly for months. (We are grateful for good doctors who later found the infection that was causing all the trouble.) Her sickness started with random, middle-of-the-night vomiting spells. We took her to several doctors who tried different remedies, but for weeks nothing worked.

I gave her all I had—my prayers, warm bubble baths, chicken noodle soup, hours of back rubs. We would crouch together on the tile of the bathroom. She would contort her small body over the toilet—me, holding back her hair with both hands, promising her it would get better soon. I wasn't always sure I believed my own words.

One night she became so violently ill that she collapsed on the bathroom floor from weariness. I was terrified, begging God to heal my girl.

Scott and I carried her to our bed and set a bucket on the floor, unsure when another vomiting episode would occur. That night, Anna lay between us, whimpering, and we stroked her hair and rubbed tiny circles into her back. I would have taken every hurt from her if I could have, and I would have asked for it double if I knew it would return health to my girl. But all the bargaining in the world didn't change things.

Before I tell you the rest of the story, I want you to know something about our Anna. She is a Giver. A few days after I created the happiness style assessment, I beta tested it on Anna. I was certain that she was a Giver. I was right. She was off the charts. This is a girl who gives in the quietest ways.

Our Anna is often teased by other kids for being shy. I have repeatedly told her that her quietness isn't a flaw or a fault—but a part of what makes her marvelous. Because she's so quiet, she listens. She sees people. She scans a room with her soft eyes and sees how to find the people who are hurt. Then, without fanfare, she finds ways to make them feel safe and valued.

Last year, I was amazed when Anna decided, after quiet and introspective deliberation, to cut ten inches off her beautiful hair so she could donate it to a child who needed a wig. I had no idea she was even considering it.

We travel occasionally to Haiti, and when we do, Anna is

the first one to bound out of bed in the morning, pull her hair into a fast bun, and run down the orphanage steps to help feed and clothe the toddlers.

But as Anna lay in bed with me, sick, some unseen illness had stolen something special from her. My quiet little Giver had nearly given up. In the dark, I swallowed the lump in my throat and thought of an idea: I'd show her pictures of the babies in Haiti.

I fetched my iPhone and found the Facebook page of the orphanage where we stayed.

"Anna, look here," I whispered. "Look at the babies. Look at their smiles, Anna."

Her whimpering faded. She swiped through the photos, and a smile swelled up from inside of her. As she viewed photo after photo, she was connecting with the part of her heart that God made so tender—the part of her that gives and loves so freely.

Fifteen minutes later, she closed her eyes with my iPhone still in her hand. I looked down at the last image she saw that night: a little Haitian boy wearing pink Crocs and the silliest grin.

Why Giving Matters to Your Happiness

Giving of ourselves freely in service to others isn't just the right thing to do; it actually lifts our own moods, even in small increments, as I witnessed that night with my daughter Anna.

Study after study draws the same conclusion: When we give to and serve others, we are on a fast track to happiness. One surefire way to be happy is to seek to make others happy.

According to researcher Shawn Achor, happiness is a renewable resource.[2] Achor suggests that we renew happiness through regular acts of giving. These acts don't have to be big. They can be as simple as complimenting people, tipping a bit extra, smiling at strangers, helping someone in need, or giving to charity.[3]

Science reveals that when we give, we reward our brains. Giving actually creates a hormonal reaction that elevates our moods and causes us to feel happy. One study shows that people who give to charity are 43 percent more likely than nongivers to describe themselves as very happy people. People who give blood are more likely to describe themselves as very happy, compared to those who don't.[4] When giving to others, Givers actually experience a mild form of euphoria, which psychologists deem "the helper's high."

Secular scientists have begun to affirm what Jesus has been telling us all along: "It is more blessed to give than to receive."[5] In the original Greek, the word we often translate as *blessed* is—you guessed it—*makarios*, the Greek word for *happy*. When we give, we are blessed. And according to God's Word, we'll be far *happier* too.

I decided to test this theory for myself on an unseasonably warm autumn day in October. I recruited my friend Jenn, a Giver, to help. I wanted to spend a whole afternoon committing random acts of kindness in our little corner of northwest Iowa. Jenn was all in. Imagine our anticipatory happiness! We had so much fun planning where we would commit our random acts. The next afternoon, we loaded up our children and stuffed the back of my Ford Explorer with baked goods, simple gifts, fresh flowers, and a gigantic sign with the words "Hey, you! You're really awesome!"

Then we got to work. We delivered banana bread to some construction workers, took cookies to an elderly couple, left

gifts on the front steps of homes where people we knew were
going through hard times. We held doors open, taped bag-
gies full of quarters to gum ball machines, and attached candy
and microwave popcorn to the movie rental box at the grocery
store—free for the taking.

Semitruck drivers wore hundred-watt smiles and laughed
when the girls held their gigantic sign at intersections. Our in-
the-moment happiness—the type of happiness people experience in real time—was off the charts.

I teared up when, after delivering flowers and a card to the
women's rehab center, a woman hugged me so long and with
such love that I forgot that the world could sometimes be a
pretty awful place. I lost it a little when she spoke these words:
"I can't believe that someone cares about us."

My favorite part of our afternoon came at the end. I'd pur-
chased a second bouquet of flowers—the last bunch in the
cooler at the grocery store. The bouquet was a hideous bunch
of overpriced daisies, featuring various shades of neon that God
simply did not intend.

But they would have to do—because I knew for sure that we
had to deliver flowers to my friend Margaret, whom I had met
while playing bingo at the nursing home. As you may recall,
during the bingo game, she had told me that if she could do life
all over again, she'd pick more daisies.

Well, she couldn't go get those daisies herself. But I knew
that I could bring them to her.

When we walked into the nursing home, the aides asked if
we would wheel the residents down to the dining hall for supper.
So for the next twenty minutes, we went room to room, looking for residents in wheelchairs who needed to be chauffeured

to dinner. All the while, I kept looking for Margaret. Finally, I found her in the corner of the dining hall.

I tapped Margaret on the shoulder and held out her bouquet. "I don't know if you remember me, Margaret. It's been a while since I've seen you. But I am really glad to call you my friend, and I want you to have these."

Tears formed in Margaret's eyes. She put a hand to her mouth and then she spoke. "I've been waiting for these," she said.

Apparently, for many months, she had been planning a "wedding." Her sister had brought her a dress, which was hanging in her room. She had a ring on her finger. But she'd been worried that she didn't have a proper bouquet. "I needed my flowers. Now I have them," she said.

It wasn't about the quality of the gift. It wasn't about me, the woman who gave it.

It was about the heart of the one who needed to know she was loved.

And that made all the difference.

Mastering the Art of "There You Are"

Giving doesn't have to cost us much. Sometimes it's as simple as how we walk into a room.

Meet Sally. She is one of those sparkly, spirited people, as if glitter runs through her veins. I met Sally at an annual retreat for the writers and staff of www.incourage.me, an online ministry of DaySpring cards. I'm on the (in)courage writing team, and at the time, Sally was one of those behind-the-scenes Givers who made sure things got done.

For two days, I observed her. (I know, I realize how stalkerish this sounds, but it was all for Jesus.) Sally would track happiness across the carpet of every room she walked into.

I told Sally what I had observed in her, and a wide smile stretched across her face. "I got it from my dad," she said. "It was about the way Dad walked into a room."

Sally told me more. Her dad taught her that when you walk into a room, you never say, "Here I am!" Instead, you say, "There you are!"

You don't actually have to *say* those words out loud, but you might. You can speak those words with your whole self.

There's a lesson about happiness and giving in Sally's words. If you want to be happier, begin with "There you are." If you want to feel a sparkle in your spirit, share a bit of your own.

That's what the Givers teach us. They show us that happiness often begins with how you walk into a room.

Givers are the "There you are" people in a world that screams, "Here I am."

Jesus: The Ultimate Giver

"There you are" is the pulsing motivation of Jesus. The ultimate Giver, Jesus believed so much in the truth of "There you are" that he came straight into our world, forfeiting the comfort of heaven for the brokenness of earth.

He fully knew the cost. The greatest Giver of all time became the greatest *Gift* of all time. Jesus walked into the room. Into the mess. Into the middle. Into the heart of things. Into our lives.

God says he loves a cheerful Giver. No one in the history of mankind has given of himself with more joy than God's own

Be a "There you are" person in a world that screams, "Here I am."

Son, our Savior, Jesus Christ. Jesus even expressed joy in his final hours on earth.

Picture the upper room. Imagine the disciples, reclining at the table, conversing over goblets and bread as the moon rose overhead. Most of the disciples were clueless, but Jesus' accusers were plotting against him even then.

This was Jesus' final supper, and it was a Passover meal. According to tradition, those gathered around the table would have eaten prescribed foods. They would have sung songs and recited a special Jewish liturgy that included hymns taken from the Psalms. The hymns were known as the *Hallel*, the psalms of praise.

The Hallel extends from Psalm 113 through 118 and includes these words:

> This is the day which the LORD has made;
> let us rejoice and be glad in it.[6]

It was likely that Jesus and his disciples recited those very words during Jesus' last hours on earth. Let that sink in for a moment. On the night Jesus was betrayed, he *sang songs of praise.* Jesus knew he was going to die, yet he uttered the words, "Let us *rejoice* and *be glad.*"

Fast-forward to Golgotha. Behold the cross, the soldiers, the spikes. See a man of sorrows who drank the terrible, beautiful cup of wrath. Meet your Savior, who "for the *joy* set before Him endured the cross."[7]

There will never be another Giver like Jesus, who laid himself down as the Gift. Jesus didn't do it with a protest. He didn't ask for anyone's applause. He didn't do it for his own glory.

He did it for the joy set before him.
The ultimate Giver? He did it for you.

Digging Deeper • • • • • • • • • • • • • • • • • •

1. Whether or not you scored highly as a Giver, God has directed each of us to give generously. He "loves a cheerful giver" (2 Corinthians 9:7). Describe a time when you felt the joy of giving—either as the giver or the recipient.

2. Jennifer addresses several red flags for Givers. Which, if any, do you most relate to?

3. Who is the most giving, generous-hearted person you know? Would you describe him or her as a "there you are" person or a "here I am" person? Explain.

4. Sometimes giving is painful. Jesus shows us just how much. Yet he endured the Cross "for the *joy* set before Him" (Hebrews 12:2, NASB, emphasis added). Reflect a moment on Christ's joy, the kind of joy that rises above the cup of wrath. Do you think it's possible for people to go through trials and still hold on to their joy? Why or why not?

CHAPTER 9

The Thinker

✌

Love the Lord your God with all your heart and with all your soul and with
all your strength and with all your mind.

JESUS IN LUKE 10:27

So you're a Thinker, are you? (Even if you're not a Thinker, read along. Chances are, you know several Thinkers, and understanding their happiness styles will help you understand and love them better. Plus, we all can learn from each other!)

Welcome to the club of the noticers, the daydreamers, and the question askers. You unashamedly push the limits of the beautiful mind that God has given you.

As a Thinker, you find supreme happiness in the contemplative work of the mind. You take delight in learning, pondering, and dreaming.

You believe this: The secret to happiness is to have the mind of Christ. You understand that the quality of your thinking is proportional to the depth of your happiness.

You are a person of many layers, so not every characteristic of a Thinker will fit you perfectly. But people tend to describe you as *curious* and *wise*, and that makes you happy.

What Makes You Tick

You love: to wonder. You love to have the space and time to contemplate. You enjoy learning something new every day. You can easily lose yourself in everything from books to the wild wonder of a June thunderstorm. You love a good metaphor and are adept at assigning meaning to common things.

If you had tomorrow afternoon free: you would most enjoy it by reading a book or listening to a podcast. You love making new and exciting discoveries and enjoy solving problems. You like to get to the bottom of things and you aren't afraid to do the arduous mind work required to get there.

You connect with God by: seeing how the earthly pleasure of learning intersects with the heavenly joy of God, who gave us the capacity to wade deep into the big questions of life. The world opens itself up to you like a wooden door to the wide unknown, and in that place you find deep connection with God.

You would be lost without: your books. For every book you finish, you add two more to the list. There's no such thing as "too many books"—only too few shelves to put them all on. It bugs you that you'll die without having had a chance to read everything you want to read and to explore everything you've wanted to explore.

People say you are: deep, inquisitive, and thirsty for knowledge. You are enthusiastic when given a problem to solve. You notice what others overlook. You have a unique way of seeing your world.

If you're at a dinner party: you enjoy a stimulating conversation. Some people may think, at first, that you are standoffish, quiet, or even a bit odd. But the truth is, you happily engage with others over a wide variety of topics, though you don't particularly care for small talk. People may say you prefer sitting in the corner with a book; that's not necessarily so. (But you likely scan your friends' bookshelves because you can learn a lot about people by what they're reading.)

Red Flags for Thinkers

You're outside your happiness sweet spot when: you forget that "the fear of the LORD is the beginning of wisdom."[1] You might also forget that God is the source of knowledge, not you. At times, you can get so lost in your mind that you neglect relationships that need to be nurtured. If you can't get to the bottom of things, you may become frustrated and obsessed, which robs you of your happiness. Ironically, we are all at our greatest risk of falling into sin or idolatry in the area where we are most wired to experience pleasure and happiness, so Thinkers run the risk of making spirituality a matter of the mind over a matter of the heart.

People who aren't afraid to speak truth to you would say: you sometimes come off as an elitist. You don't want to admit when you're wrong. You get frustrated with others who don't see things your way.

You can feel unsettled when: you don't have the answer. This makes you feel incompetent, and you fear that you'll look stupid.

You feel you've let God down when: someone points out an error in your reasoning—particularly when you're talking about God. You may also feel you've let God down when you watch your friends connect more easily with others than you do because they are natural Relaters or Givers.

You feel shame when: people think you are antisocial or cold. People may misunderstand what happiness means to you because your happiness is a quieter, inside happiness that doesn't always express itself in bold, outward ways. As a result, some people think you are chronically melancholic even when you are actually quite happy.

You shame others when: they don't share your thirst for knowledge and problem solving. People frustrate you when they don't "get" you or misunderstand your unique way of seeing the world. As a result, you might make them feel stupid or shallow.

How to Be the Happiest You

You will be in your sweet spot when: you are consciously aware that your search for a higher understanding always leads to God. You will grow in wisdom and happiness when you remember that God is the source of both. Your happiness will increase when you are able to use that wisdom to help other people understand their world—through art, writing, music, and the spoken word.

You will stay in your sweet spot when: you remember that, as much as God loves your mind, he also wants your heart.

You will hold on to your happiness when you realize that some mysteries can never be solved and you won't get to the bottom of everything until you are in heaven.

Avoid shaming yourself by: realizing we are all created differently. What brings you happiness may make your Experiencer and Relater friends wonder if you've gone mad. For instance, there's nothing wrong with you if you would prefer to watch a documentary on Saturday night instead of going to the block party with the Relaters in your life.

Avoid shaming others by: realizing they were created for their own sweet spots too. Just as they have something to learn from you, you have something to learn from the Doers, Experiencers, Relaters, and Givers. Like you, they were created in the image of God. When people don't care to analyze or perceive the hidden mysteries of this world the way that you do, go easy on them. Their happiness styles differ from yours, and such intensive analyzing might exhaust them rather than make them happy.

You can love the Thinkers in your life by: giving them what they want most of all—space to learn. Oh, and maybe more bookshelves. The Experiencers dream about being trapped on a tropical island for a week. The Relaters are already planning next week's shindig. But the Thinkers in your life dream about getting locked inside a bookstore overnight.

The Story of a Thinker

This boy's story began unhappily. He came into the world prematurely in a stone farmhouse in the English countryside. No one expected him to live. His father died three months before he was born. They named him Isaac, after his dad. Isaac was very sick, very small—but also terrifically tenacious. Despite all odds, the boy survived.

But the story doesn't take its turn toward happiness quite yet.

When he was only two, this boy's mother deserted him, so his grandparents raised him. Most accounts suggest that his childhood was unhappy. The boy had no mother to sing him lullabies or rock him when he awoke at 3 a.m. He had no father to teach him how to farm the fields or gaze upon the stars in wonder.

I can't say for sure, but I picture the boy having to fight for a happy life, gasping for it like lungs gasp for air. Here's where he found happiness: in books; in his mind's ability to marvel; and in the canals of his own brain, which carried him on great intellectual adventures. In his quest to find answers, he also found the footprints of God.

Isaac had a fantastic imagination to match his hungry faith. He crafted kites, not so much to play, but to see which proportions flew best. Those who knew him said he was hardly ever seen without a pen in his hand or a book in front of him.

Isaac loved school. But in his teen years, he was called by the family away from school to work on the farm. It's not an understatement to say that Isaac made an awful farmer. When he was supposed to be mending fences, he was reading. The farm's sheep trampled the neighbor's corn because he didn't keep an eye on them. Once, while leading his horse up a hill by its bridle, he was so engaged in a book that he didn't notice the horse slip out of its bridle and run off.[2]

Here's why: Our young Isaac wasn't a farmer; he was a scientist.

And he grew up to become one of the world's greatest. You know him as Isaac Newton. Yes, the guy who invented calculus and formulated the law of gravitation.

Isaac Newton was a Christian who met God through the lens of his own curiosity, in the depths of the school library, and inside his wild imagination. He even found God at his own fingertips. "In the absence of any other proof," he said, "the thumb alone would convince me of God's existence." One author said of Isaac, "He was happiest when alone with books, papers, experiments, and ideas."[3]

But despite the complexity and magnitude of his achievements, Isaac always possessed this childlike quality: he remained in awe of the mystery of our world. He once said, "I don't know what I may seem to the world, but as to myself, I seem to have been only like a boy playing on the seashore and diverting myself in now and then finding a smoother pebble or a prettier shell than ordinary, whilst the great ocean of truth lay all undiscovered before me."[4]

Isaac Newton was a Thinker. He found happiness inside the terrific brain granted to him by his Maker.

But look. You don't have to discover the law of gravity to be a Thinker. You don't have to love calculus—or even understand it.

If you take delight in the wonders of this God-created world, if you enjoy learning something new every day, if you daydream and ponder, you might be a Thinker too.

If you highlight your pages and scribble in your margins and enter some secret wormhole when you crack the spine of a book, you might be a Thinker.

If you stand under the moon on the night of a lunar eclipse, astonished and captivated by the unusual aligning of events that made it all happen, you might be a Thinker.

If you aren't afraid to ask the eyebrow-raising questions and dig uncommonly deep to search for the answers, you might be a Thinker.

If you assign value to the drifting leaf, if you ponder the depth of the sea stretching out before you, and if you notice what others overlook, you might be a Thinker.

If you get lost in your mind, only to find the fullness of God—yes, you are likely a Thinker.

Jesus Loves the Thinkers

Jesus told us to love the Lord with all our heart and all our soul. *But he also told us to love the Lord with all our mind.*

To all the Thinkers out there, reading these words today: Do you know what a treasure you are? Maybe you do. Maybe you proudly wear the badge of a Thinker. You know how you were wired, and you are comfortable that being a Thinker is woven into the fabric of your soul.

But for some of you, today might be the first day you've been told that your inquisitive, wandering, wild mind doesn't make you weird; it makes you wonderful. It isn't a flaw. It's a part of what makes you a masterpiece.

Maybe you've been called absentminded. Maybe you've endured happiness shaming as a Thinker. Maybe others wanted you to come to the church meet-and-greet, but you wanted to curl up on the couch with a bowl of sriracha almonds and binge-watch *Planet Earth*. You've always been a daydreamer, and your mom used to snap her fingers in front of your nose to

*Your inquisitive,
wandering, wild
mind doesn't
make you weird;
it makes you
wonderful.*

get you to eat your peas. Maybe the grown-ups wondered why you were spaced out, when you were actually plucking thoughts from thin air. You *were*, in fact, paying attention. You were noticing. You were using the uncommon gift of folding up this noisy world and tucking it away for later because you wanted to re-hear and re-see what the rest of us have been missing.

The world opens itself up to you just as it did for the psalmist when he could hardly take it all in: "When I consider your heavens, the work of your fingers, the moon and the stars, which you have set in place, what is mankind that you are mindful of them, human beings that you care for them?"[5]

Oh, Thinker. You are mystifying and marvelous. You are the one who stops to read every plaque underneath every museum exhibit. You love to learn and explore. You chase hard after your electric mind when it invites you to enchanting places.

You don't need a dinner party or a roller-coaster ride to find happiness. All you need is your one beautiful mind. And if the rest of us would slow down enough to listen to you, you might tell us what you see. Or you might paint us a picture. You might pray the most thoughtful prayer that makes a lump rise up in our throats. You might write a poem or teach us a card trick.

We all know that we can love Jesus with our actions and our hearts. But Thinkers like you show us what it means to love Jesus with our curiosity. Thinkers like you unashamedly push the limits of the beautiful minds that God has given each of us. This gift of the active mind is not yours alone, for we've all been given a mind, but you show us how to cultivate its pastures.

All of us—whether we are Experiencers, Givers, Relaters, or Doers—have much to learn from the Thinkers. Thinkers show us that our questions aren't curses, but are pathways to God's answers. Thinkers show us that, when we ponder and reason the things of God, we aren't trying to outsmart him. We're becoming more like him.

"Come now, and let us reason together, saith the Lord."[6] A Thinker's propensity toward curiosity isn't an attempt to defy God. It's a way to know him.

If you are a Thinker, perhaps you can relate to the apostle Thomas. And perhaps you bristle when he gets a bad rap with that tired moniker "doubting Thomas." Jesus didn't berate Thomas for his questions or for his inquisitive mind. Jesus answered Thomas's questions with an uncommon tenderness. And because of those brave questions, we all benefit from the answers that Jesus gave him.

Thomas asks Jesus in John 14:5, "Lord, we don't know where you are going, so how can we know the way?"

Without that question, we wouldn't have the stunning revelation of John 14:6. Jesus responds to Thomas with one of the most-quoted verses in all of Scripture: "I am the way and the truth and the life. No one comes to the Father except through me."[7]

Jesus didn't merely tolerate Thinkers. He made a place for them at the table. Jesus loves the Thinkers.

The Way of the Thinker

For many of us, our thoughts and our questions have awakened in us a great love for our Savior. The happiest relationship I've ever known began when I engaged the power of the mind. Only after satisfying my intellectual curiosity about the Christian faith was I able to enter into a relationship of trust with Jesus.

I had to open my mind in order for God to open my heart.

Many Thinkers might use another word to describe themselves: *Contemplatives*. The word itself has a holy ring to it, doesn't it?

For good reason. It comes from the Latin roots *com* (meaning "with") and *templum* (meaning "temple").[8] When we contemplate with "the mind of Christ,"[9] we are *com templum*, or "with the temple." Thinkers have a way of peeling back the gauzy curtain of heaven to see backstage into the deeper things of God.

From where the rest of us are standing, it may seem like the Thinkers—off in their own worlds, tugging at heaven's veil—have turned their backs on us. To the contrary, they are practicing the presence of God. And if we stick around long enough, they will happily turn back around to tell us what they see.

You don't have to be a smarty-pants to be a Thinker. You just have to be curious.

God grabs the attention of the Thinkers, and Thinkers respond to God's whisper by seeing with their whole selves—their eyes, their hearts, and their intellects—thus drawing nearer to the heart of Christ.

My friend Yettee is a Thinker. I'm guessing she has a high IQ, but what I treasure most about her mind is its high sensitivity to God's whispers. "When I'm asked to share about my hobbies, I always list these three: gardening, reading, and thinking," Yettee says. "I love to wonder. I want to know why the bird made the nest and why he made it that way. When I was a kid, I wanted to know why the grass was green and whoever thought to call it green anyway."

Thinking makes Yettee happy. Yettee's friends joke that she sees beauty in the strangest places—like roadside ditches. Where others see weeds, she sees the creativity of God shooting heavenward.

Yettee's ability to respond to God's whispers is almost child-like. It reminds me of a scene from the book *Charlotte's Web*. In the tale, a pig named Wilbur is made famous by a spider named Charlotte, who weaves words about Wilbur in her web.

One day, Mrs. Arable, another character in the book, asks the family doctor, "Do you understand how there could be any writing in a spider's web?"

"Oh no," Dr. Dorian says. "I don't understand it. But for that matter I don't understand how a spider learned to spin a web in the first place. When the words appeared, everyone said they were a miracle. But nobody pointed out that the web itself is a miracle."[10]

Thinkers are the Dr. Dorians of the world. They see the ordinary miracle of the web, as if always viewing it for the first time with a child's eyes. They don't demand that a spider spin a word within the web; the web itself is the miracle. And they become engrossed.

One modern-day scientist has a word for this—a word for that moment when you get so engrossed that you lose track of time and place. The word is *flow*. Flow is what happens when you're in the zone—the happy zone—and when hours pass like minutes. It's a kind of heightened focus when you are immersed in tasks that provide you with knowledge or fulfillment.[11]

Thinkers may not realize they are in the happy zone until after they are done with their thinking-associated tasks.

That's the way it was with Isaac Newton. At Cambridge, he became known for missing meals. He would become so engrossed in his thoughts or in his studies that he would forget to eat. (I have Thinker tendencies, but I can guarantee you I would *never* forget a meal. I plan all of my days around food.)

Thinkers might not even identify happiness as a core motivation of their thoughts and actions. They might not consciously consider that they are happy in those moments of flow because they are really not paying attention to themselves at all (nor to their appetites, apparently).

My friend Holley took the happiness style assessment and scored highest as a Thinker. "I'm in that state of flow sometimes, and I'm not really aware of myself," she said. "It's only looking back that I can say, 'Those were some of the best moments of my day.'"

Quite often, Thinkers aren't merely thinking for thinking's sake. Thinkers have purposes beyond the accumulation of knowledge. Some of the Kingdom's most famous Thinkers have used their thinking power to make the world a happier, healthier, more livable place. They are using their minds to make scientific discoveries, write books, sculpt statues, and compose symphonies.

Bach, for instance, had a great and creative mind, and he harnessed that mind power to create some of the world's most famous musical scores. But in the end, his compositions were never for him alone. He included these three initials at the bottom of many of his musical compositions: *SDG*. The initials stand for *Soli Deo gloria*, a Latin phrase meaning "Glory to God alone."

When Holley engages in thoughtful activity, she is more than a Thinker. She sees herself as part Relater, part Giver, and part Doer. She says she's thinking about the people who will read her books or blog posts or the people who will hear her speak from the podium.

"Even though I'm alone in my thoughts, my readers are

there. Real people are there. Jesus is there. A whole community is there. I'm doing my thinking on behalf of other people. I'm still people centered, just in a different way," Holley said. "It can be challenging to have your happiness style be Thinker. It feels, at first, like I should have a happiness style with more obvious impact. It can feel like I'm too solitary. But that's not true at all. When I am thinking, I feel like all of my people are with me—all the time. I have to remember that because I can feel guilty thinking, *If I really cared about people, I should be a Relater.* But that's not true. Thinkers love people too."

Those guilty feelings are common among Thinkers. Our culture has many built-in ideas about how to make a happy moment: *Go to the movies! Play a card game! Invite the whole neighborhood over for dinner!* But the kinds of activities that our culture encourages actually make some people feel less happy. We can end up forcing ourselves to do things we don't really like in the name of happiness, but if we do so, we often end up feeling unhappier than we were before.

Of course, there are times when we have to leave our comfort zones in the name of being decent human beings or simply to stretch ourselves. Though we might not like the dinner party, our loved ones might. And if we are going to love people well, we need to help them maximize their own sweet spots of happiness even if they differ from ours.

Like people in all of the happiness styles, Thinkers have to guard against a form of happiness idolatry. A Thinker can step outside the place where earthly pleasure meets heavenly joy. Thinkers can become so consumed with their thoughts that those thoughts become idols. Thinkers can chase so hard after knowledge that they forget who first granted it.

Isaac Newton understood that. At age nineteen, he made a list of sins, including this: "Setting my heart on money, learning, pleasure more than Thee."[12] Isaac Newton apparently understood the pitfall of worshipping the gift of the mind rather than the one who gave it.

Apart from God, our intellectual pursuits become a maddening chase. With God, they become a fantastic way to bring him glory. *SDG.*

The Quality of Our Thought Life

I am a Doer. But ever since I was a child, I have found great contentment by nurturing my own sweet spot of thinking-based happiness.

When I was a girl, I would skip along the sidewalks of our little Iowa town, headed for the library, which was open three days a week. I would check out my books and walk all the way home, reading as I walked—perhaps dangerously unaware of traffic. I would climb up the limbs of our backyard trees with my books or hide on the roof of the house, where the shingles burned hot beneath my legs.

I could hear the children below racing by on their Schwinn bicycles. I knew that somewhere out there, I was probably missing out on games of tag and hide-and-seek. So be it. I was happily consumed by Madeleine L'Engle or Judy Blume.

Even now, there are nights when I would rather watch a documentary or listen to a podcast than meet up with friends for a girls' night out.

But some of the most powerful thinking isn't an intellectual pursuit at all. It's a spiritual one.

The quality of our thought life is a tremendous indicator of the quality of our happiness. The Bible says that God can transform you into a new person "by changing the way you think."[13] That's why studying God's Word is imperative for all people—Doers, Relaters, Experiencers, Givers, and Thinkers. When we hide God's Word in our hearts and minds, it serves us in times of crisis.

Puritan Thomas Brooks put it this way:

If you would but in good earnest set upon reading of the holy Scriptures, you may find in them so many happinesses as cannot be numbered, and so great happinesses as cannot be measured, and so copious happinesses as cannot be defined, and such precious happinesses as cannot be valued; and if all this won't draw you to read the holy Scriptures conscientiously and frequently, I know not what will.[14]

God renews minds through the power of his Word and the work of his Holy Spirit. As believers, we have everything we need to rescue our joy in the hardest times of our lives.

Let me tell you about a Thursday night, one very pain-filled night, when I was standing in the dimly lit sanctuary of my country church. I had come there to pray with a few friends due to an overwhelming set of circumstances in my life. Suddenly, I felt such a deep sense of panic that I thought I couldn't breathe.

It was an anxiety attack. I'd never had one before, but I knew what was happening when it hit me. I was nearly knocked off my feet by the overwhelming sense of panic that I felt, even in the solitude of God's house.

I gripped the wooden pew in front of me while my heart raced and my throat closed around itself. I felt despair and a complete loss of control. I couldn't find the words to pray, but years of thoughts and meditation on God's Word let me know for sure that God was there.

My thinking was saving me, even then.

My mind had stored up its own happiness—from God's truth—kind of like the way a person keeps a savings account to fall back on in hard times. When I couldn't breathe, I remembered who God said I was and I remembered who God said *he* was. When I couldn't breathe, it was as if God was breathing for me. He breathed Scripture into me, God-breathed Scripture.

Bible verses formed a line of defense in my mind, pushing back enemy forces. My mind recalled God's promises. I remembered a happiness that I once held, and I knew for sure that joy was recoverable based upon the evidence of God's Word. The verses came to mind, flip-book style.

Don't be afraid.

Lo, I am with you always.

My peace I give you.

Nothing can separate you from the love of God that is in Christ Jesus our Lord.[15]

In that panicky moment, I found some peace. I was unable to fully grab hold of happiness, for happiness felt slippery right then. But I felt a peace coming on. And based on the trustworthiness of my Father, I could believe that I would find my joy again one day because God does not lie.[16]

For months after that anxiety attack, I prayed through tears for my circumstances to change. Two years have passed now, and the circumstances are almost identical. God didn't answer my prayer to change my circumstances, but he is doing something else: He is changing me.

There are days I wish I could go back to "how things were." There are days I still pray that God will work a miracle and change the circumstances that led to that first anxiety attack.

But even when he doesn't answer my prayer the way I want him to, so be it. Blessed be his name anyway. He is always good and he is always working. And he is my happiness.

My racing, anxious mind is calmed when I rest inside the arms of Christ. My unhappiness is eased when I ask God to give me the mind of Christ. The great rescue of a great Savior brings happiness to my heart and mind that is unsurpassable by anything I can imagine.

The best thinking we will ever do is when we think on the things of Jesus. When we allow him to pervade our thoughts, our imaginations, and our dreams. When we see Creation and behold his goodness. When we step outside of ourselves to sneak a peek behind the holy veil, to steal a view of heaven. When we, like Isaac Newton, marvel at the thumb and know that God is real. When we, on Sunday mornings, stand before the wooden cross nailed to the wall and behold the place where Jesus had thoughts too—thoughts of you and me.

Even from the cross, Jesus taught us by example how to set our minds on heaven, when all around us the world may waver and buckle. Think about the good things, the apostle

Paul tells us: "Finally, brothers and sisters, whatever is true, whatever is noble, whatever is right, whatever is pure, whatever is lovely, whatever is admirable—if anything is excellent or praiseworthy—think about such things."[17]

Think about the things that make you smile, that give you a forever hope, and that remind you that it's going to be okay—that you're going to make it. Knowing that happiness is not only permissible, but is possible through God, makes even the hardest days more bearable. And it makes the best days infinitely brighter. Because for everything he has given us—every treasure on earth, every moment we enjoy, every delicious meal, every exquisite sunrise, everything—God himself surpasses it all. Jesus Christ himself is our happiness.

Now that is something to think about.

Digging Deeper • • • • • • • • • • • • • • • • •

1. Whether or not you scored highly as a Thinker, God has given each of us the ability to wonder, dream, and learn. When was the last time you felt true happiness in learning something new—whether in school, in a book, from a podcast, or in a Bible study?

2. Jennifer addresses several red flags for Thinkers. Which, if any, do you most relate to?

3. How comfortable, or uncomfortable, are you with questioning the things of God? If you can, describe a time in your life when you wanted God to satisfy your intellectual curiosity about the Christian faith.

PART 3

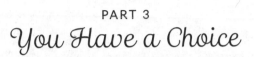

You Have a Choice

In this section of *The Happiness Dare*, we will:

Learn how just five minutes a day devoted
to happiness can retrain the brain

Understand the four main obstacles to happiness
and find a way around them

Learn that, while Jesus cares about our happiness,
he also sits with us in our tears

Find new ways to fight for happiness during hard times

Understand that no matter what our
"happiness set points" are, we have the ability
to boost our happiness

Learn how our happiness can
change the world

CHAPTER 10

Five Minutes to a Happier You

～

The art of being happy lies in the power
of extracting happiness from common things.
HENRY WARD BEECHER

This is the part of the book where I would do just about any-thing to jump through the pages, hold you by the hand, and say, "We can do this, friend."

You and I took the dare. And now we're being called to live it. That is exhilarating—and scary.

Exhilarating, because we know the exciting truth that hap-piness is not only permissible by God but is achievable through him. We have learned that happiness isn't separate from our holiness but is a part of it. We understand that there is an actual sweet spot of happiness for each of us—where earthly plea-sure meets heavenly joy. We see how we were hardwired by God himself to encounter the pleasures of this world as Doers, Relaters, Experiencers, Givers, and Thinkers.

But happiness is also scary because it leaves us feeling

vulnerable. If I'm happy now, will it last? Is tomorrow "jinxed" if everything is going well today? Does my happiness have value in a world that increasingly gives voice to the cynics—or will I just be an annoying, overly merry irritant? Dare I be happy on days when my news feed is filled with links to school shootings, refugees fleeing for their lives, and politicians squabbling? If my life is already filled with blessings, am I selfish to want more happiness than I already have?

I wrote this book because I needed this book. I needed to know if my happiness mattered. And if it mattered, how could I go about finding it and then living it out in a place pulverized by pain and heartache?

This is what I know today after reading numerous studies, books, and scientific research and then applying tested principles in my own life: Happiness is a potent force. Happiness is tied to more love, better health, more generosity, increased productivity, more compassion, happier families, better workplaces, and more creativity. Our happiness doesn't end with us. People can "catch" our mood. Grumpiness is contagious. So is happiness.

I don't know what you're facing today. I don't know why you picked up this book in the first place or why someone slipped it into your hands. Maybe happiness feels like an impossible dream for you. Maybe your happiness was snatched away by a diagnosis, a pink slip, divorce papers, a death notice, or a friendship that turned ugly. Maybe you're like me—half-afraid that the happiness you presently have will evaporate in one skinny minute. We've all seen how that can happen.

If we've ever needed each other on this Happiness Dare, it is now.

Let me tell you a story to show you why. This is a story for all of us—no matter how happy or unhappy we are today.

Why We All Need a Ladder toward Happiness

A man fell into a hole as he was walking down a street. The walls of the hole were so steep he couldn't climb out. So the man in the hole began to cry for help.

Soon a doctor walked by and he heard the man's cries. The doctor wrote a prescription, tossed it down the hole, and walked away.

Before long, a priest walked by and heard the man calling out. "Father, can you help me?" the man asked. The priest wrote a prayer, threw it in the hole, and walked away.

Finally, a friend came along. And the man asked the friend for help. The friend then made a brave, bold move: He jumped into the hole. The man who had been trapped was aghast. "Why'd you do that? Now we're both stuck here!"

The friend said, "Yes, but I know the way out because I've been down here before."[1]

This story is a parable meant for all of us—no matter how happy or unhappy we are. Right now, all of us are in one of two places. We are either stuck in a hole, trying to find a way out. Or we're walking along the street, seeing holes all around and hearing only voices.

As I sit here typing these words, tears fill my eyes. I think about the people I know who are stuck in great holes of unhappiness. And I think about the people who happily helped me out of mine.

I was stuck in a hole for many years in my early adulthood.

My hole was the shape of doubt. I have known no greater unhappiness than I knew during those years when I felt sure that God was a liar—if he even existed at all. I didn't believe the story of Jesus' death and resurrection. I was afraid that the whole Bible was a sham. But I was too ashamed to cry out for help. The walls of my hole were too steep for me to climb out on my own. And if there was a God, well, he didn't seem to care. I was so terribly angry at an invisible deity who was supposedly all-knowing yet didn't bother dropping me a rope.

I thought I might die there in the dark.

God didn't drop me a rope, but he sent a friend who knew how to build a ladder. He sent someone who knew the terrain of the hole I was in, someone who understood doubt. And that friend helped me build a ladder so I could climb out. That ladder was fashioned out of my friend's prayers, her genuine interest in my life, and her willingness to take me as I was—doubts and all. I was able to get out of the hole because she was willing to jump in it with me.

When I finally stood on the rim of the hole, I could see with startling clarity that God had done more than send a friend during that season. He'd done the unthinkable: Long ago, he'd sent himself.

This is the gospel. God stood at the edge of a hole and he heard people crying for help. But God didn't write us a prescription and throw it down the hole. He didn't pray and then walk away. He made the boldest, bravest move in human history: He jumped into the hole. Jesus forfeited heaven and lived on the inside of every hole, every mess, every valley you could imagine.

Scriptures tell us that Jesus "experienced it all himself—all the pain, all the testing—and would be able to help where help was needed."[2]

Jesus gets you. He knows the steepness of all the walls in all the holes. He is uniquely equipped to hear your cry, to jump into the most treacherous hole, and to help you find the way out. Jesus is the way out. Jesus is the ladder.

Where are you today?

Are you inside the hole, ashamed to cry out like I was? Or maybe your voice is hoarse from crying out so long, and all you've got is a pile of prescriptions and prayers at your feet. Friend, Jesus is right there with you, building you a ladder. Jesus is daring you to climb the ladder, one rung at a time. And your fellow dare takers are with you too. You are not alone in that hole.

Happiness is the ladder that draws you from the deep. Small steps, friend. You can do this.

Or maybe you've already been rescued and you're living in freedom up on the street. You have been blessed and you can't get over the extravagance of the blessing. Yet your heart hurts because you recognize that there are people in great big holes of unhappiness. You might even feel guilty when you look at the happy life you're living. Friend, Jesus might be calling you to do the brave, bold, ridiculous thing: Jump in and help a friend build a ladder. Share the happiness you've found in Jesus and let that happiness be a real way out of the hole. Someone is waiting for you. This is paramount to the Happiness Dare. We've got to be bold enough to jump in—all in—to share what we've found with someone else who needs us.

All of us need ladders out of the holes we find ourselves in, and those ladders are built one rung at a time, one moment of happiness at a time, until we find ourselves standing in the light. I believe it with all my heart, and that's why I'm writing this book to you.

Yes, it's hard. Happiness is not for the scaredy cats. To find happiness, we've got to muster our courage and fight for it. We've got to chase after it. We have to be the ladder builders who don't stop building until we meet the fullness of our happiness in heaven.

It takes courage to wake up every day and stalk authentic happiness, especially when we're being sold a faux version. The prevailing message in the world is that you can only be happy if you're sporting the right style, wearing the right size, driving the right car, and living with the right kind of husband and the right kinds of well-behaved kids who don't have one another's fingernail marks scratched into their forearms—all while living a glitter-dipped life.

That message is built on the myth of *scarcity*—the false belief that there is only so much happiness to go around. The myth of scarcity blinds us to the abundance we've been given and keeps us from being grateful for what we already possess.

We know better, don't we? We've all come this far. We have decided that genuine happiness is worth fighting for—and that there's more than enough for everyone. We don't have to hoard our happiness. There's more at stake than just our mood. Our happiness is a mighty weapon against the angst and bitterness of this world.

There's another great big reason to fight for happiness: Our delight matters eminently to God. John Piper writes: "To the extent that we try to abandon the pursuit of our own pleasure, we fail to honor God and love people. Or, to put it positively: The pursuit of pleasure is a necessary part of all worship and virtue. That is: The chief end of man is to glorify God by enjoying him forever."[3]

We are made for happiness—not only for our own delight, but supremely for God's.

We have been shown the way. We've seen how God uniquely created us as Doers, Relaters, Experiencers, Givers, and Thinkers (or a beautiful combination of those types) as a way to "enjoy him forever." We've learned how God created us for sweet spots of happiness right where we are. And we've seen how Jesus modeled happiness in his own life. Christ is the ultimate Doer, Relater, Experiencer, Giver, and Thinker.

But reading a book about happiness is not enough. Hoping for happier days ahead is not enough. We have to put happiness into practice, because the enemy is working against us. The enemy knows how our happiness can draw us closer to God, make us more generous, deepen our relationships with others, and advance the cause of the gospel.

Now it's time to get to work.

Like our family friend Ron tells us, "You may have evicted the devil from your life. But he's out in the parking lot doing push-ups."

We've got to do some biblical boot camp. We need a heavy regimen of spiritual push-ups. We've got to exercise our muscles and fight for the happiness we were made for.

The good news?

It starts with just five minutes every day.

The Spiritual Discipline of Happiness

What if I told you that you could begin to build a ladder toward your sweet spot of happiness with five minutes of focused happiness work every single day?

That's where you begin. Start small. Invest five minutes every day toward building a durable ladder of happiness, no matter what else is going on in your life, no matter how busy you are, no matter how sad or horrible you feel. Even if you don't know if you can get out of bed today. This is central to the Happiness Dare: Invest five minutes in seeking the kind of pleasure that brings happiness to your heart and brings glory to our God.

"Think about such things"

Begin with five minutes of intense focus on the things that you know to be true about Jesus. Start in the Scriptures and connect with Jesus as Healer, Protector, Savior, Provider, Friend, and the Originator of true happiness. Do what God instructs by focusing—for five minutes—on "whatever is true, whatever is noble, whatever is right, whatever is pure, whatever is lovely, whatever is admirable—if anything is excellent or praiseworthy—think about such things."[4]

Faith is a proven and powerful weapon against unhappiness, and it's a weapon that nonbelievers simply don't have. We would be foolish not to use it and even more foolish if we didn't tell others that faith is an effective defense in a world where the enemy wants to steal our joy.

According to research, faith works when it comes to happiness. Studies show that people who attend church regularly get a happiness boost.[5] Psychologists say one reason is this: Religious beliefs give people a sense of meaning. Even in the midst of tragedy, we have hope because we know that our trials build character. And, in fact, the Bible says we can actually experience joy in the midst of trial—an unthinkable idea were it not for the hope of Jesus Christ. Paul writes, "We can rejoice, too, when we run into problems and trials, for we know that they help us develop endurance. And endurance develops strength of character, and character strengthens our confident hope of salvation."[6]

This mind-set helps people make sense of tragedy, suffering, and loss, according to Catherine Sanderson, a psychology professor.[7] That means that spending even five minutes a day reading Scripture can change things. Meditating on God's truths is more than a good spiritual discipline. It changes your outlook. Praying, studying God's Word, and pondering "whatever is lovely, whatever is admirable" have a palpable effect on your level of happiness.

Start with five minutes and watch your ladder grow, one rung at a time.

Enlarge your sweet spot

Building your ladder doesn't end there.

You could also commit five minutes every day to enlarging your sweet spot of happiness. Nourish your happiness by using what God already gave you.

Are you a Doer? Pick two to three easy tasks (such as making your bed or straightening the piles on your desk) that you can finish easily. You no doubt have a to-do list, but don't forget to take five minutes to write a "done" list to highlight what you accomplished.

Are you a Relater? Call up a friend. Send an encouraging text to your sister. RSVP to the dinner party. Flip through old photo albums and linger on the faces of people who have loved you well.

Are you an Experiencer? Make a playlist for your hike this

weekend. Invest five minutes in a stroll around the yard. Post an old picture of a past vacation on Facebook and experience the residual happiness that comes with the memory. Take five minutes to see what events—like farmers' markets or concerts—will be happening in your area this coming weekend. Dig the picnic basket out of the pantry and make plans with the family.

Are you a Giver? Take five minutes to write a card to a person on the church's prayer list. Send a check to your favorite charity. Drop a few canned goods off at the food pantry on your way to the post office. Pay for someone's coffee at Starbucks. Drop a few extra coins in a parking meter.

Are you a Thinker? Spend five minutes crafting a poem. Read a short passage in a book. Listen to NPR. Take a brisk walk outside to give yourself the space you need to contemplate. Look out the window and simply wonder about things without feeling the least bit guilty over the work that must get done today.

Five minutes. And then five more, and five more. We are building ladders of happiness here. When we direct our actions toward what makes us happy, our minds' pleasure centers are activated.

Take your thoughts captive

Maybe you've heard the Native American legend about wolves. It's a parable that perfectly illustrates the way to happiness. According to the story, the grandson of an old Cherokee chief asked his grandfather, "Why is life so unhappy?"

The wise chief thought for a moment and then asked his grandson to listen to the wolves howling in the distance.

The boy listened.

The grandfather continued: "A fight is going on inside me.

It is a terrible fight and it is between two wolves. One is evil—he is anger, envy, sorrow, and regret. The other is good—he is joy, peace, love, and hope. This same fight is going on inside you—and inside every other person too."

The grandson thought about that for a moment and then asked his grandfather, "Which wolf will win?"

The old chief simply replied, "The one you feed."[8]

Which wolf are we feeding?

When we feed our minds with happy moments and happy thoughts, we are not falling for some hokey gimmick. We are feeding the right wolf. We are storing up happiness. We are taking "captive every thought to make it obedient to Christ."[9]

This takes discipline—not unlike the discipline we need to be more patient, peaceful, self-controlled, and kind. No one would disagree that we need discipline, through the power of the Holy Spirit, to access all the fruits of the Spirit. We also have spiritual disciplines of prayer, Bible reading, worshipping, fasting, and serving others. Today let's begin the spiritual discipline of happiness. We can take our thoughts captive and make them obedient to Christ.

If we don't give those five minutes to God, who will gladly take them all? The enemy himself. The enemy specializes in wanting to mess with us. The enemy of your happiness doesn't want you to have the mind of Christ. He wants you to have the mind of chaos.

When we focus on good thoughts, it's as if we are taking a "Sabbath in the brain," according to Dr. Caroline Leaf.[10] Without a brain Sabbath, she says, we will ruminate and obsess. We will surrender our minds to negative thinking. We will compare and obsess and have inner freak attacks.

"You are free to make choices about how you focus your attention, and this affects how the chemicals and proteins and wiring of your brain change and function," Dr. Leaf tells us.[11]

Science is catching up with what God has said for a really, really long time. More than two thousand years ago, Paul penned these words: "Be transformed by the renewing of your mind."[12] Science now agrees with what Paul wrote to the Romans. Our minds can be renewed. (More on that in the next chapter.)

I know what you might be asking yourself: *Can five minutes a day really make a difference?* Experts say yes, it can. Research reveals that five to sixteen minutes a day of focused, meditative thoughts increase the chances of a happier outlook on life.[13] In five to sixteen minutes, science says, you can be happier.

Start with five. Just five. And begin to alter your brain.

With the Holy Spirit in you, you can direct your mind toward happiness and away from anxious or bitter thoughts.

What Stands in the Way of Happiness

The final chapters of this book will help you learn how to take control of your mind. We will tear down the obstacles that stand in the way of our happiness and apply fresh principles to help us live freer and happier lives.

There are so many words we tell ourselves about ourselves that undermine our happiness. Here are the four most common statements that get in the way of happiness:

1. "This is just the way I am." Many people falsely believe that they are condemned to unhappiness and thus can't ever become happier than they already are.

2. "If I could just be like her." We give away so much of our happiness when we compare ourselves to others and hold ourselves up to fictitious standards.
3. "My life circumstances make happiness an impossible dream." Many people lose the will to fight for happiness when their worst nightmares come true.
4. "If only I had _____." We miss out on our happiness when we wish for what could be while neglecting to be grateful for what already is.

I have been held hostage by all four of those statements. But when I took this dare, I began to tell myself a different story. I adopted four new principles, which you will find in the chapters ahead. Those principles—based on science and Scripture—can help you build ladders out of all sorts of holes.

Unlike happiness styles, which differ from person to person, these four principles apply to every one of us. We can all strengthen and stretch our happiness muscles by practicing them. The more we repeat them, the easier they will become, the more natural they will feel, and the more happiness we will experience.

To help us begin applying the principles, each of the next four chapters ends with five-minute exercises (which I call "happiness hacks"). But don't stop there: I hope you'll use the happiness hacks as a springboard for your own ideas on how to practice each happiness principle.

Will you finish strong with me?

One of the biggest obstacles standing between us and sustainable happiness is this: We think that if we can't have it all now, we can't have it at all. We think that if we don't see immediate results, then it's never going to happen for us.

We've got work ahead of us. Before we head onto the field, can we all huddle up to high-five one another and cheer each other on? Let me tell you a story that is giving me great hope about happiness, even in the face of great obstacles.

As I was finishing writing the last chapters of this book, I watched two people living out the Happiness Dare in real time: my parents.

For the last year and a half, my dad had been battling a broken ankle that led to a horrible infection, which began to eat away at his bone. A few days ago, my dad had part of his right leg amputated.

There was a moment—one that still leaves me a little misty-eyed—that unfolded a few hours after the surgery at Mayo Clinic.

All of us kids were there, gathered around Dad's hospital bed with Mom. Two nurses were stringing up an IV bag and pushing buttons on a monitor.

And Dad . . . he just looked around the room at all of us. He wore this smile that you could see in his eyes as much as on his lips. It was a smile that revealed an inner peace.

He looked each one of us in the eye and thanked us for being there. He talked about blessings. He mentioned all that he was grateful for—family, togetherness, love, life, the prayers of friends and strangers, and the chance to start again. He recalled what the surgeon had told him a few days earlier: "Don't think of this as losing a leg; think of this as getting a new leg and moving on."

Then he asked for a Dairy Queen Snickers Blizzard, which I promptly fetched.

I know that "looking on the bright side" comes easier for

some folks than others. I also know that Dad is a generally optimistic person. Like me, Dad's happiness set point is set to sunny. But I also know that there are certain valleys where finding joy can be really, really hard—even for an optimist.

Yet Dad has been showing all of us what it looks like to find the patches of light, even in the shadows.

I believe Dad's response comes from a lifetime of drawing closer to God and putting into practice the four principles we'll address on the coming pages. I have not always handled my own problems with that kind of grace, but I am learning from watching my parents.

One of the things they are teaching me is how to find the happy in the hard. Sometimes it seemed like the worst possible news . . . was the very news Dad got from the doctors. It would have been easy for him to give up.

Yet he is demonstrating what it means to stick to the Happiness Dare on the hardest days. He finds humor inside a hospital. He cracks jokes with the doctors. He hugs us and tells us how much he loves us. He orders more Blizzards.

But you know what else? Dad isn't afraid to cry. He isn't scared of the sadness. He isn't frightened of his own wide-swinging emotions, or ours. That's part of what makes Dad's happiness real and durable: his willingness to embrace the breadth of emotions that swirl within each of us.

The day after Dad's leg was partially amputated, I took the elevator down to the basement level to buy a sandwich in the cafeteria. When the elevator opened, I heard music. A man was playing the grand piano in the lobby, and another man was singing "This Little Light of Mine."

I stepped into the lobby, where a crowd had begun to gather.

All of us were on our way somewhere else, but all of us had stopped.

I sat on the floor while tears streamed down my cheeks.

And this is what I knew in that moment: Sometimes the obstacles to happiness seem insurmountable. But the happiness of Jesus is unstoppable.

We will often find happiness in places we never thought to look, like the lobby at Mayo Clinic. There we were—patients and daughters and moms and grandpas and nurses and therapists—all shuffling from place to place. A lot of us were lugging our heartache and worry with us, chins sort of pinned to our chests, eyes to the ground.

But then, up rose a song. *"This little light of mine, I'm gonna let it shine."*

When none of us could sing, someone brought us a song. Two people jumped into the hole with us. They didn't throw down a prescription; they didn't give us a halfhearted prayer.

They jumped into the hole. With a song, they built a ladder.

The man singing invited us to join in, so that's what we did. Some of us cried through the words, "This little light of mine." But we sang anyway.

This is what it means to fight for happiness on the hardest days, no matter what obstacles lie before us.

Friend, believe that it really can be different. Build one rung at a time—five minutes a day—and watch your ladder rise.

You may have setbacks. You may need do-overs. There will be days when you feel that, while the rest of the world is celebrating on cloud nine, you're living on cloud two.

I'm not telling you that beginning to build that ladder will lead you straight to cloud nine. But I will promise you that with the Holy Spirit, you have everything you need to be a happier you.

Look up. See the silhouette of a ladder. Then rise, friend. This is your time to shine.

Let it shine, let it shine. Let it shine.

Digging Deeper •••••••••••••••••

1. Jennifer relayed a story about a man who fell into a hole. Today do you see yourself as being in the hole and needing a ladder out? Or are you out of the hole but feeling the nudge to climb down into someone else's to help that person build a ladder?

2. Studies have shown that possessing faith can be a weapon against unhappiness. Would you agree or disagree? Why?

3. Read Romans 12:2: "Be transformed by the renewing of your mind." Science now confirms the truth of that Scripture. What can you do, in five minutes each day, to begin to renew your mind and alter your thoughts toward happiness?

4. Jennifer tells a story of finding happiness in an unlikely place—the lobby of Mayo Clinic. Share a time when you found happiness unexpectedly, perhaps in the midst of a trial.

CHAPTER 11

The Principle of Small Daily Gains

～ᵧ⌐

HAPPINESS HIJACKER:
This is just the way I am.

HAPPINESS BOOSTER:
*Little by little, I can become happier
by changing the way I think.*

Confession: I am prone to assume that the absolute worst is about to happen.

If I read a news story about a statistical increase in farm-related accidents, I suddenly freak out and psycho-dial my farmer husband to make sure he's alive. If I don't hear back immediately, I begin planning his hypothetical funeral.

The other day, I had a strange tingling in my thumb. So I googled my symptoms, and in less than ten minutes, I determined that I had either had a stroke or was possibly the first-ever sufferer of finger cancer.

It doesn't stop there. I can go completely bonkers some nights. After the lights are out, I sometimes huddle under the covers, wide-eyed and whispering to my husband, "Honey? Do you hear that?" I don't want to admit this to you, but I sometimes imagine that I hear zombies or serial killers outside the bedroom window. Those are the nights I am certain that I've watched too many apocalyptic shows on Netflix.

Good grief! I can waste so much time and energy assuming the worst.

But we do this sometimes, don't we? We can look at a limited set of facts and make assumptions that lead to the worst possible outcomes.

If that's you, you might be relieved to know that you are not crazy. You are totally normal. The human mind is skewed toward negative feelings.

That's because all people have what's called a *negativity bias*. Even the most optimistic person you know has this bias. Science tells us that our brains are wired in a way that causes us to assume the worst—a killer in the bushes, a monster under the bed, and so on. There's a historical basis for this: We humans used to be prey. We had to be hypervigilant, as if our lives depended on it, because they did. Our negativity bias served us well. It kept us alive if there was a tiger hiding in the tall grass. We could end up as the tiger's midafternoon snack if we dismissed the sounds coming from the grass as simply "the wind."

Our negativity bias is still helpful in certain situations: when we want to cross the street or when we are deciding whether to park in an unlit lot. Our negativity bias is a built-in warning system. But our negativity bias can often be problematic. Benign situations can be misunderstood as real threats.

Your negativity bias is the reason you remember insults longer than praise. It's the reason you obsess over the mistakes you've made. If one hundred people say something about you and only one of those remarks is negative, you are most likely to remember the negative remark because of your negativity bias. I used to cover politics when I was a news reporter, and all of us in the newsroom knew that the politicians who used negative ads against their opponents generally had more memorable campaigns than those who aired positive ads about themselves.

Our negativity bias can breed unhappiness.

If we assume the worst in life instead of the best, our pessimism can spread faster than a terminal case of finger cancer.

That can all sound rather hopeless. But it's not.

Many people falsely believe that they are condemned to unhappiness and thus can't ever become happier than they already are. They believe this about themselves: *This is just the way I am.*

But that's not entirely true. None of us are "just that way." Neuropsychologist Rick Hanson says that all people have the power to overcome their negativity bias. If you've ever taken an exercise class, you know that you have to train your muscles to handle more sit-ups or more laps around the track. In the same way, we have to train the muscles in our brains to steer away from our negativity bias and toward a richer happiness.

During my own Happiness Dare, I have been keenly aware of my negativity bias and have worked to control it rather than letting it control me. I have taken active steps toward positivity by applying Solomon's words: "For as he thinketh in his heart, so is he."[1]

One way to overcome our negativity bias is to let ourselves linger over positive experiences. When we linger, we are allowing ourselves to sit with good feelings. We are hitting the pause button on our lives so we can take time to appreciate something delightful. Instead of racing onward to the next task after completing a project, Doers can linger for a few minutes to celebrate what they've accomplished. Experiencers can swipe through their iPhone photo libraries to remember the good times they had last week. Thinkers can take five minutes to journal about their latest discoveries.

Science tells us that when we linger—even for a few extra seconds—we are actually helping rewire our brains. Lingering helps our brains transfer positive feelings from our short-term memories into our long-term memories, says Hanson, author of the book *Hardwiring Happiness*. He says:

> People tend to be really good at having that beneficial state of mind in the first place, but they don't take the extra 10 seconds required for the transfer to occur from short-term memory buffers to long-term storage. Really get those neurons firing together so that they wire this growing inner strength in your brain.[2]

Maybe you're like me. Maybe you wouldn't describe yourself as a naturally good lingerer. For a moment, consider how quickly you move past celebrating an accomplishment at work because you see the stack of papers still sitting on your desk. Think how fast you brush off a compliment instead of letting yourself linger long enough to internalize the kind words.

We need to linger longer and better.

Linger at the back of the movie theater when the credits are rolling to soak in the happy ending. (That's residual happiness.)

Linger at the table with your husband and let the dinner plates sit a few more minutes. (That's in-the-moment happiness.)

Linger over your plans for tomorrow's girls' day out. (That's anticipatory happiness.)

Linger over the kind words that someone texted you this morning. Linger in the warm bath, under the dome of stars, or above the earth at 30,000 feet while staring out the airplane window.

Linger over God's promises to you. Linger in prayer. Studies show that people who meditate have measurably thicker brains in the areas that are important for well-being.[3]

In the spirit of full disclosure, my mental exercises—while effective—have revealed high levels of spiritual ADHD. Case in point: A few days ago, I drove Lydia to school for a jazz band rehearsal. It was before dawn, and after dropping her off, my thoughts became anxious and jumbly.

Traveling the dark and deserted road home, worry became my friend. Questions like these put a stranglehold on my thinking: *How will I get it all done today? What will I do about the unresolved conflicts in my life? What if it all falls apart?*

If my brain had fingernails, it would have gnawed them all off. (I guess that would mean that my brain would also need teeth. I digress.) Worry swelled up to commandeer spaces in my brain that I was unwittingly surrendering to unhealthy and unproductive thinking. It was as if my negativity bias had gulped down four energy drinks when I wasn't paying attention.

Just then, I turned the corner to head east back to our house. The sun had begun to rise with its first burst of ruby on the edge of the earth. In the presence of God's new mercies, visible in that thin line between heaven and earth, I did one of these . . . *siiiiiighhhhhh.*

I lingered.

Right then, I realized that in the miles previous, my brain had been feasting on its negativity bias. And I remembered that I had the power within me to exercise my brain toward positivity.

I felt the familiar words of Jesus stir in my heart: "Come to me, all of you who are weary and carry heavy burdens."[4] Again, *siiiiiighhhhhh.*

I decided to devote the next five minutes to lingering. I slowly drove up our long country lane, barely inching along, with the gravel crunching under my tires. I pondered only the things of Jesus. I thought only of the truth of his Word.

Well, that's not exactly true. Step inside my brain to see how it really went down:

> *Dear God, you tell me not to be anxious about anything, and I know that you mean what . . . oh my word. I totally forgot to send the e-mail to Anna's teacher yesterday, which reminds me, my in-box is sobbing digital tears under the weight of all the unanswered e-mails, and did I remember to respond to my editor's request? I'M THE MOST IRRESPONSIBLE AUTHOR EVER! . . . Oh, wait. Hi, Jesus. Back to you, so sorry. Anyway, like I was saying, I know that your yoke is easy. Yoke. Yoke. Yolk! Egg yolk! Need more eggs. Gotta get to the store today, or my people will have nothing to eat but the heels of stale bread along with the dust at the bottom of the Cheerios box, and . . . Oh, Lord, where were we?*

This is an unattractive—but very real—picture of what it looks like to exercise my prone-to-wander brain. I'm still trying to work out this lingering thing.

By the time I parked my car in the garage, my belligerent brain had caught up to my heart's honest desire to take God at his word. It took work and focused attention. But inch by inch, the Holy Spirit took back the ground that I had surrendered to worry and fear. It wasn't easy. My mind is super stubborn and has lived under the authority of my negativity bias for a long time. Because of that, it wants to retread old ground. My thoughts want to wander away from Jesus.

I want to "fix" stuff. But Jesus says, "Fix your eyes on me."

That morning, I walked into the house and sat down at my desk. I still had the same set of circumstances. I still had the same long to-do list. Unresolved conflicts hadn't been resolved. But I was looking at everything with a renewed mind—with the mind of Christ. In five minutes, I felt a renewed sense of relief, contentment, and happiness.

That's the power of our minds. We do not have to be victims of our circumstances. We do not have to be held hostage by worry-filled thought patterns and negativity biases. As we've seen, our minds are actually renewable.[5]

This isn't a sweet little metaphor. It's an actual fact. Some of the most rigorous research in neuroscience now reveals what God has been saying all along. Our brains have what scientists call neuroplasticity. That's a fancy word that tells us we are literally capable of changing how our minds operate. The brain is malleable. When we linger on happy experiences or positive truths, these thoughts become encoded. Neural connections strengthen. The brain undergoes actual physical change.[6]

All of us are capable of increases in happiness. We aren't doomed to live under the oppressive state of our negativity bias. We really can teach our old brains new tricks.

The Tetris Effect

Our minds are not unchangeable masses of cells and gray matter. Our brains are molded significantly by what we put into them.

Let me give you an example. Back in the early 1990s, my friend got a Nintendo Game Boy for Christmas. One afternoon, she slipped a cartridge into the slot and handed me the Game Boy. The game was called Tetris. In the game, colorful blocks of different shapes would fall from the top to the bottom of the screen, and the player would rotate and maneuver the blocks so they'd fit together tightly at the bottom. As the game progressed, the blocks would fall faster. I loved that game. I still do!

That night as a teenager, I went to bed, and my dreams were completely overrun with blocks falling from the ceiling of my bedroom. In the dream, I raced around my bed to place the blocks on my pink comforter before they stacked up and broke through the ceiling of our house.

The next day, my friend and I laughed about my dream. She had been replaying the game in her mind, too, even when the Game Boy wasn't in her hands.

Turns out, dreams about Tetris are an actual thing. It's called the *Tetris effect*. The effect occurs when people spend so much time on one activity that the activity invades their thoughts and dreams.

Researcher Shawn Achor was the first to tie the Tetris effect to increased happiness. Harnessing the power of the Tetris effect, people can reprogram their brains toward happiness, says Achor, author of *The Happiness Advantage*. By training our brains to constantly scan for and focus on positive events and moments, he says, we can boost our happiness.[7]

For many years, my brain was under the influence of a more insidious type of Tetris effect. I grew up as a happy, optimistic child. As I've mentioned, all of us have a happiness set point, and mine was genetically set to cheeriness. That changed gradually when I grew into adulthood. I began to assume the worst in everything and everyone. I had become a news reporter and I spent years witnessing people at their worst when covering robberies, murders, child-abuse cases, and arson. My brain was retraining itself toward negativity. I questioned every politician's motive and was suspicious of any corporate executive who "declined to comment." I doubted everyone and trusted no one.

One of my professors famously told us, "If your mother says she loves you, double-check it." That's pretty decent advice if you want to build a healthy dose of skepticism as a reporter, but over time, living with that level of mistrust can build a crust of cynicism over a person's heart.

Trust me, Jesus had a *lot* of work to do when he began to reprogram my mind. I doubted the existence of God for many years. I put Jesus in the same category as comic-book action figures: strong and mighty on paper, but pure fiction and utterly useless in times of need.

Even now, as a devoted follower of Christ, my mind requires regular reprogramming to counterattack the years of negativity. But this Happiness Dare is helping. Applying the Principle of Small Daily Gains, which we will discuss in the next section, is changing me from the inside out. With even a few minutes a day of focused thoughts aimed at positivity, my neurons have started firing toward happiness and wholeness.

Small Steps, Small Daily Gains

"This is just the way I am." These seven words are standing in the way of happiness for a lot of us. I've met a number of people who assume they are so predisposed toward unhappiness that a happiness boost is impossible.

By applying the Principle of Small Daily Gains, however, we can change the quality of our thought lives. One thought at a time. One lingering moment at a time. One five-minute interval at a time. Over time, our small daily gains accumulate to make a measurable difference—a difference far greater than I ever would have guessed.

Consider the eye-opening work of Sonja Lyubomirsky, who has spent most of her research career on the study of human happiness. In her book *The How of Happiness*, she reveals that our happiness consists of three parts. To summarize:

- Fifty percent of our happiness is governed by genes. We all have a genetic set point for happiness, much in the same way we have set points for our metabolism, intelligence, and athleticism.
- Ten percent of our happiness is dictated by life's circumstances. Those can be good circumstances or bad ones—for example, getting the job you always wanted, losing a beloved pet, finding someone to spend the rest of your life with, coming home to discover that the oak tree in your front yard fell through the roof of your house. This is a surprisingly small percentage. It offers scientific proof that the key to happiness isn't primarily in changing our circumstances.

- A full 40 percent is left to us. Here lies the key to increasing our happiness. This 40 percent is within our ability to control and includes what we do and how we think. Here's where we have the power to become happier through intentional activities.[8]

"If we observe genuinely happy people, we shall find that they do not just sit around being contented," Lyubomirsky writes. "They make things happen. They pursue new understandings, seek new achievements, and control their thoughts and feelings. In sum, our intentional, effortful activities have a powerful effect on how happy we are, over and above the effects of our set points and . . . circumstances."[9]

We have a lot of room to maneuver within that 40 percent window. This is where we intentionally find ways to maximize the holy-happy place where our earthly pleasures connect with heavenly joy. Here we can push back the tidal wave of negativity by changing how we think.

We can literally get a happiness upgrade by thinking happier thoughts, by making small daily gains. What might that look like for you?

Doers: Engage in purposeful work in your backyards, in your cubicles, and at your sewing machines and artists' easels. Linger over the good work you've accomplished. Instead of letting your negativity bias go into overdrive, dwell on what you've done well rather than hyperfocusing on the one negative comment you heard from the committee chairwoman or your coworker.

Relaters: Plan a game night this weekend with family and friends. When it's over, linger over the fun and meaningful experiences you've had with the people you love. Record the memory in a journal. Shoot off a text to someone to let her know you appreciate her. If it's been a hard day, scan the previous twelve hours for signs of relational positivity. Ask yourself: *Who made me smile today?* When you do that, you're making the Tetris effect work to your advantage.

Experiencers: Even on your hardest days, step outside to marvel at the beauty of this grand old world. Linger upon the handiwork of God. Take a walk and proactively scan for good stuff. Repeat as needed, and observe how your neuroplastic brain responds. Plan your next big adventure and let your mind experience anticipatory happiness.

Givers: Send a care package to your college kids, rake the neighbor's yard, take an extra five minutes to pray for the people listed in your church directory, or mail that card you've been meaning to send for the past week. Think of the last time your giving made a difference, then linger over that thought for a boost of residual happiness.

Thinkers: Even if you're busy, crack open a book for a few guilt-free minutes and get lost in the mystery. Take five minutes to pick up the phone and make a lunch date with another Thinker who "gets you." Ask your Facebook friends to suggest a new podcast and listen to the podcast on the way to and from work.

All of us, together, can push back against every negative thought. We can make small daily gains in that 40 percent window by expanding our sweet spots in the ways that God has uniquely wired us.

Let's start with five minutes. And then? Maybe we can try ten minutes. Then twenty. Warning: the renewing of one's mind toward happiness is addictive behavior. The more time we devote to positivity, the more fuel we give our brains to establish new neural pathways. We make our brains stronger and better—and happier.

This is the Principle of Small Daily Gains: taking one step at a time, one action at a time, one five-minute interval at a time to change yourself from the inside out.

How the Principle of Small Daily Gains Works

Several years ago, I took a different kind of dare that illustrates how the Principle of Small Daily Gains works.

My sister-in-law Aimee challenged me to run a half marathon as a fund-raiser for lymphoma and leukemia research. I had five months to train before we ran the route along the streets of Lincoln, Nebraska. The finish line was the fifty-yard line of the Nebraska Cornhuskers football stadium.

The obstacles between me and that finish line seemed, at times, insurmountable. Some days, I regretted taking her challenge in the first place. I lugged around my not-enoughs: *I'm not disciplined enough. I'm not athletic enough.* Of everyone on our half marathon training team, I was the slowest. Furthermore, a year earlier, I had suffered a leg injury in a collision on an icy highway when an oncoming car crossed into my lane, hitting me nearly head-on.

But I took the challenge, and it started with a single first step. My first time out running, I simply ran to the mailbox at the end of our country lane and then I walked back to the house. The next day, I ran a bit farther.

Before long, I was running three or four miles at a time, interspersed by periods of walking. In the middle of my training, there were real obstacles: injury, self-doubt, tired legs, burning lungs, exhaustion, even boredom.

But on a May morning in Nebraska, it happened. There we were, among eight thousand other runners, shivering while warming up and waiting for the starter's gun. A woman ahead of me wore a T-shirt with this phrase written on it: "Three months ago, this seemed like a great idea." *How fitting,* I thought, as I nervously bounced around.

Then the starter's gun fired. The words of my coach rang in my ears: "You've already earned the medal; you just have to cover 13.1 miles to claim it!"

Even as I ran the race, I had to think about the next step and then the one after that. That's what we can all do in life: Take the next step. Run to the mailbox. Apply the Principle of Small Daily Gains.

The good news is, we're not doing this alone. We are together on the back of the lion, Jesus Christ. He's already done all the hard work, securing for us the promise of eternal happiness and promising us moments of pure joy before we reach the final destination.

You aren't "just this way." You are more, so much more.

Because of Jesus, you've already won the medal. You just have to cover a few miles to claim it.

Digging Deeper • • • • • • • • • • • • • • • • •

1. *This is just the way I am.* How have you seen this Happiness Hijacker at work?

2. Would you describe yourself as a good "lingerer," allowing yourself to hit the pause button and reflect upon the

positive experiences or accomplishments in your life?
Or do you quickly move on to whatever's next?

3. Jennifer told the story of running to the mailbox on her
   first day of training for a half-marathon. She encouraged
   you to think about the next step and then the one after
   that, rather than getting overwhelmed by the long
   journey. How can you "run to the mailbox" today? What
   small step can you take to boost your happiness?

Five-Minute Happiness Hacks

The Principle of Small Daily Gains

1. **Host a five-minute linger session for yourself.**
   Allow your brain to sit with good feelings. Stop
   to appreciate a finished task (Doers), a chat with
   your friend (Relaters), the great time you had last
   night (Experiencers), the way the neighbor smiled
   when you shoveled her walk (Givers), the poetic
   turn of a phrase (Thinkers).

2. **Make the Tetris effect work for you.**
   Take five minutes to scan for the good in your
   life. You'll do yourself a favor today, while also
   retraining your brain to look for the good in
   the future.

3. **Write a "done" list.**
   This list will mark what you've already accomplished, leading to residual happiness.

4. **Journal for five minutes.**
   Focus on the positives in your life—past, present,
   or future—to counterattack your negativity bias.

5. **"Run to the mailbox."**
   Instead of obsessing over the long race ahead, set
   and meet small goals. Small steps matter!

6. **Give yourself the satisfaction of doing one
   five-minute good deed per day.**
   My nephew Brennan works as an automobile
   salesman. Every morning he cleans the parking lot
   of litter—not because it's in his job description,
   but because it makes him happy to help.

CHAPTER 12

The Principle of Good Enough

ᕐ

HAPPINESS HIJACKER:
If I could just be like her.

HAPPINESS BOOSTER:
Instead of wishing for her life,
I will find happiness in my own.

A few weeks ago I saw a photograph of someone's office on her blog. It was *gorgeous*. No clutter. Natural light. No crap stacks. The woman had arranged fresh flowers in a vase on her desk. There were no computer cords visible anywhere. I wondered: Did everything run on batteries and solar power?

I lowered my gaze to my desk and then scanned the teetering piles atop my filing cabinets. My whole office was in need of major reconstructive surgery. Important documents were buried. Scraps of scribbled notes were lost. Gremlins had tied all of my cords into knots. There was a snowdriftish layer of dust behind the computer.

Because I am a Doer, I rubbed my hands together, and with visions of that other woman's desk, I happily went to work. I may have even whistled.

Hours later, I had rearranged all my papers, thrown away two garbage bags full of files from my cabinets, sorted all my books by color on the bookshelves, and washi-taped several hand-lettered prints to the wall. Voilà!

I stood back to admire my work, but what I saw left me feeling forlorn and hopeless. I immediately saw the flaws: *This isn't good enough. It doesn't look like that picture at all. IT WILL NEVER LOOK LIKE THAT PICTURE!* (Insert maniacal, shifty-eyed emoji.)

I fussed some more, rearranged another stack of books, and then I had a revelation. Myself said to myself, *Girl, seriously. Stop. You are certifiably insane. Cut yourself some slack. Be you. Let go of your hyperfussiness and live your actual life.*

This is what it looks like when a woman believes one of the four major happiness-killing statements: "If I could just be like her."

This statement is a myth. It is at the root of so much unhappiness among men and women. We battle perfectionism, insecurity, comparison—or a combination of all three.

The result is this: We give away much of our happiness when we hold ourselves up to fictitious standards that no one can meet. When we try hard to be someone we're not, thinking it will make us happy, we end up more cheerless than we were in the first place.

Here's the good news. If you want to be happier, you can stop wishing for someone else's life and discover happiness in the one you have. You can stop striving to be "just like her" and instead live into the fullest version of yourself.

You can live by the Principle of Good Enough, instead of rat-racing your way toward the A-plus.

Say it with me: Good enough is good enough.

Believe me, I'm preaching to myself. I've written countless blog posts and book chapters and keynote addresses about those pesky not-enoughs, the tiring life of perfectionism, and the joy-robbing habit of comparison.

That day in my office, I remembered the Principle of Good Enough. And I'm so glad I did. Because I stopped fussing and got moving on the work that God actually called me to do in that office. I'm a Doer, and I take great delight in living a life of purpose. But I am a writer Doer, not a *Better Homes and Gardens* decorator Doer.

I have to say: I still admire and appreciate the beauty of that other woman's office. But that's *her* office space, and mine is mine. Mine will never be Instagrammable. I can celebrate her beauty without letting it prescribe something about who I should be.

When we chase perfection, we'll never finish the tasks before us. When we see only our own inadequacies, we'll never feel capable of doing what God has called us to do. And when we compare, we'll always find ourselves in want of more. All three of those behaviors leave us decidedly unhappy.

Sometimes the only way to enjoy your *own* beautiful life is to apply the Principle of Good Enough. The happiest people understand that good enough really *is* good enough.

The Poison of Perfectionism

A few days after I had that fit in my office, I posted about it on my Facebook page. I confessed my feelings because I knew that so many other people were giving away their happiness by striving toward invisible standards.

Hours later, I checked in on Facebook and noticed that a man had chimed in with this comment: "With that kind of advice, you would make a horrible football coach. Can you imagine a coach inspiring his players at halftime with a speech that 'good enough is good enough'?"

He was right. I would make a horrible football coach and not just because I don't know a blitz from a bootleg. I would make a horrible football coach because I'm not looking to win trophies anymore. I'm here to enjoy my time on the field.

I wasn't always that way. I used to be a win-at-all-costs kind of girl. But that life never gave me the happiness that I envisioned. Instead, it left me in desperate need of a nap. I am learning to live by the Principle of Good Enough.

Maybe you are already living by that principle. If that's you, congratulations! You already know the happiness of living as if good enough is good enough. You can move along to the next chapter, and the rest of us will find you there in a few minutes.

But many of you are in need of a fresh reminder that your flawless performances can't give you the happiness you imagine.

I bring you great news today and an invitation to the club of good enough. In this club, we can stop chasing the next best thing and learn that our lives don't have to be perfect to be fulfilling.

Research tells us that our little club is on to something. Psychologist Barry Schwartz says there are two types of people in the world. Satisficers settle for "good enough." Maximizers are always going for the gold.

Guess which type is happier?

Maximizers actually *do* earn more in the workplace, but they tend to question every decision they make. They suffer from FOMO (fear of missing out). They are always raising the bar and face regular disappointments when they fail to reach the invisible standards they set for themselves—and for others. They are actually less satisfied with their jobs than satisficers.

Satisficers, on the other hand, settle for less than perfect. They might not earn as much as their maximizer friends. They might not lead their football teams to the Super Bowl. But they know what it means to cut themselves some slack. And in the end, they are considerably happier.[1]

Culture is selling us a different promise. We're taught to believe that happiness correlates with working our tails off. If we're parents, we might mistakenly pass those beliefs on to our children. We might push them so hard that no one is satisfied until they are at the top of the class, the star of the team, the first chair in the band.

Perfect performances don't boost our happiness, at least not long-term. Often they deflate it. Perfectionists have a hard time enjoying their successes because there is always something better they could have done. Failure isn't an option, so the fear of failing undermines creativity. Fear of failure keeps people from taking risks and embracing new challenges. Perfectionism also makes people averse to critique, even helpful critique.

No matter what your happiness style is, perfectionism can rob you of happiness.

Experiencers, for instance, might plan the perfect vacation for the family, anticipating the joy the children will experience at Magic Kingdom or Legoland. But then, no amount of fairy dust will stop the wailing and gnashing of teeth of children who enter full meltdown mode during the hour-long wait for the Peter Pan ride. One sweaty, overtired kid pukes on It's a

Small World, and you are certain that your six-year-old will need therapy at age twenty-five on account of your taking him into Disney's Haunted Mansion. Suddenly you are suffering from Disney World Syndrome—your perfect vacation has been hijacked by unrealistic expectations, and the seven dwarves have walked away with your happiness. Hi-ho, hi-ho.

Relaters feel the pressure too. They have high expectations for an amicable Christmas dinner, for instance. But out of the corners of their eyes, discerning Relaters see who is glaring at whom over the water goblets—and they can't for the life of them figure out why *everybody can't just get along, for heaven's sake!*

Doers? Yes, they suffer from high expectations too. In fact, settling for good enough can feel more daunting than striving for perfection. We Doers hold ourselves to unreasonably high standards. (Side note: God didn't tell us to live like slackers. While we are not called to perfectionism, we are called to excellence. "Don't just do the minimum that will get you by. Do your best. Work from the heart for your real Master, for God."[2])

But let's jump off the perfectionist train before it takes us to Crazy Town. The Bible doesn't say to do *the* best. It says to do *your* best. It doesn't say that my office needs to look like the office from that other woman's blog. It doesn't say that my productivity should match my best friend's. As Disney princess Elsa once said, we can "let it go."

Sometimes that means that I'll learn to settle for good enough and find that I'm happier than I would have been if I had busted my butt angling for perfection—a perfection that could never be reached anyway.

That can be hard for us to believe when we're fed the message that the top finishers are the happiest. But check out this fascinating study: A few years ago, researchers discovered that Olympic bronze medalists were actually happier than silver medalists. The reason: Silver medalists were more inclined to compare themselves to the gold medal winners. Bronze medalists generally compared themselves to someone who didn't get a medal.[3]

I'm not suggesting that we all start comparing the sheens of our medals as a way toward happiness. But that study reveals a lot about happiness. Good enough is good enough—crap stacks and all.

The Poison of Inadequacy

So many people are robbed of happiness when they assume that real happiness lies in richer, skinnier, smarter, funnier versions of themselves.

In 2014, I wrote *Love Idol*, a book that helps women free themselves from their feelings of inadequacy by reminding them that they are preapproved in Christ. In the months after that, I took that message to women across the United States. And no matter where I went, I discovered how women are more alike than we are different. Almost every woman I met—regardless of income, race, or marital status—has struggled with feelings of inadequacy.

As I stood before a group of women during one of my first speaking engagements, I had to fight back my own insecurities. Was my hair right? Did I dress right? Did I have something stuck in my teeth? Why did I wave my arms around so much when I talked? Would they find me knowledgeable enough? Would they wish they had hired another speaker like Lisa Bevere or Christine Caine?

God knew about my self-doubt, too, and he kept repeating this one message into my heart: *I didn't ask you to be her. I asked you to be you.*

Our feelings of inadequacy make us anxious and rob us of the happiness that God intended for us to have. True happiness is available while living the fullest versions of ourselves.

I have a confession to make. I sometimes forget all of that. I am in need of constant reminders from God that I am loved as I am, even in the everyday moments of life.

For instance, I do the stupidest things to make a good impression on people. On the week of a dentist's appointment, I floss diligently, hoping that I can magically make up for months of laziness and not disappoint my sweet dental hygienist. If you're coming over to my house, I might make housecleaning an Olympic sport, sprinting across the living room, hurdling over the coffee table toward the toy closet, and high-diving from the stairs to deliver the laundry before you ring the doorbell. When I have a doctor's appointment, I scrounge through dresser drawers to find the lightest-weight outfit I own, so that I might see a more favorable digital reading when I step on the doctor's scale.

For the love of Pete.

At least we are in good company.

All through Scripture, we see our faith heroes go head-to-head with their own not-enoughs. Their self-doubts drove them to despair, anguish, and outright begging—the opposite of happy.

Do you remember what Moses said to God when God called him to a mission? He said, "Lord, please send someone else to do it."[4] Moses didn't feel eloquent enough.

And then there was Gideon, who certainly didn't feel strong

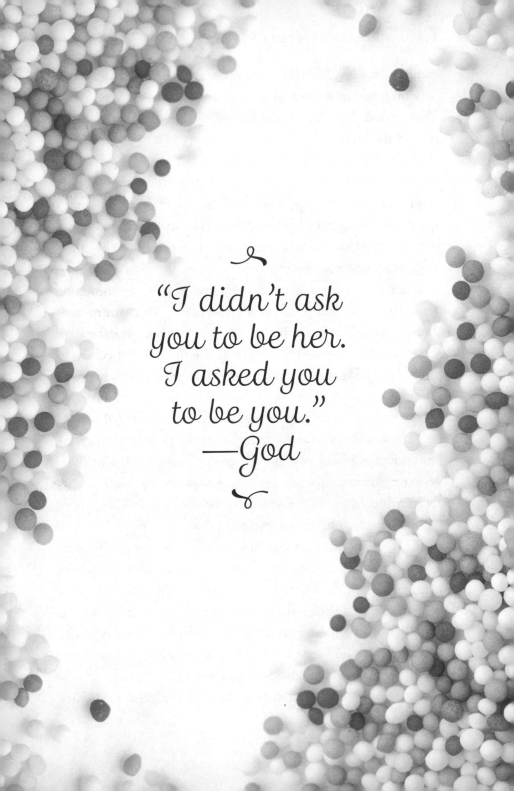

"I didn't ask
you to be her.
I asked you
to be you."
—God

enough. Imagine his pleading eyes when he begged the Lord: "*Me*, my master? How and with what could I ever save Israel? Look at me. My clan's the weakest in Manasseh and I'm the runt of the litter."[5]

It doesn't end there.

Sarah thought she was too old. (Not young enough.) The woman at the well thought she was too sinful. (Not holy enough.) Zacchaeus thought he was too short. (Not tall enough.) And a poor widow with two small copper coins may have thought she was not worth enough.

But God had an answer for every one of those not-enoughs. He gave Sarah a child. He gave the woman at the well a new life. He gave Zacchaeus his company at dinner. And he gave the poor widow some high praise. Imagine their happiness in knowing that God had faith in them, even when they didn't have faith in themselves.

He has an answer for our inadequacies too.

Maybe today you don't feel smart enough. Or mother-in-law enough. Or wife enough. Or skinny enough. Or Christian enough. Or maybe, dare I say, *happy enough*?

Imagine God, whispering these words to you: "You aren't enough *in you*. But you are enough *in me*."

That's his answer for our inadequacy. He gives us himself. That's a terrific trade and the source of my greatest happiness of all.

Jesus didn't die for *pretend* you. He died for *real* you. We are not capable of anything in our own strength. We are not self-sufficient. We are God-sufficient. If we could have done it on our own, we wouldn't have needed Jesus.

God is calling us to live inside of *his* adequacy and *his* strength. God's power is made perfect in our weakness—not in our performances or our perfection.

Sit inside of that truth for a minute and let the happiness of it overtake you.

When I think about who Jesus says I am, I am the happiest version of myself. When I remember that God loves me as-is, I am simply overjoyed. When I lose myself in the Principle of Good Enough, I realize I don't have to do it all. Because Christ *is* my all in all!

Do you remember the Sermon on the Mount and how Jesus spoke of *makarios*, the Greek word that means "happy"? On the hillside, he spoke those words to people who may have been feeling pressed down by their own not-enoughs. He spoke to the meek, the poor in spirit, and the persecuted.

Jesus said: "Happy are you . . ." His people's inadequacies didn't disqualify them from *makarios*. It gave them a front-row seat. Jesus didn't say we'd find happiness in pulling ourselves up by our own bootstraps. We find happiness by living as pure-hearted, merciful children of God.

"Be happy and glad," he said, "for a great reward is kept for you in heaven."[6]

The Poison of Comparison

The other day, I ran across an old photograph. It was taken a couple of months after I started dating Scott, the man I'd eventually marry.

In the photo, Scott has his arm around my waist. I'm smiling, but it looks like a smile I'm not feeling on the inside. I remember why. I was so self-conscious, hoping to impress my new boyfriend. Before our date, I stood in front of my mirror with the mascara wand, silently pinpointing every flaw. I didn't like how my hair turned out. I felt fat in the plaid skirt I'd picked out. I wanted to look beautiful, but felt frumpy compared to my girlfriends.

When I saw the photograph twenty years later, I took pity on that young woman. She was beautiful. She was falling in love. She had a great job offer in front of her, and a few days later, she would take it. But she was so preoccupied with her insufficiency compared to every other woman that she was blinded to who she really was.

Looking at the photo, I thought of how so much of our happiness is given away because we miss the inherent beauty of our own lives. We operate out of our desire to be as capable, smart, organized, and valued as someone else.

So much of our own unhappiness is rooted in assuming that someone else is living the happy life we want. We start to calculate how much it will cost us to get there: how much hustle, how much earning, how many calories burned, how many promotions.

Comparison is robbing us of our happiness.

I see it on Facebook and at the city park. I see it in the blogosphere and in the churches, school gymnasiums, and playdates in the park. We're comparing our waist sizes, Fitbit steps, square footage, IQs, yard greenness, ab flatness, Scripture memorization goals, kids' report cards, marriages, and island vacations.

All of our comparing is turning our pursuit of happiness into a strenuous sprint in which we never reach our destination.

Let's halt the cycle of comparison—you and me. Let it begin with us.

Let's say another woman gets what we want: a promotion, a new house, a pat on the back. If we want to supersize our happiness, we can actually be genuinely happy for her. Our happiness is automatically limited if we can only be happy for the people closest to us. Think how our happiness might grow bigger when we begin to "rejoice with those who rejoice."[7] We can rejoice with our families and best friends, but perhaps we can also rejoice with the people we have seen as competitors in our career fields and communities.

Let's go first. Let's begin to look at other people with the eyes of Christ. Let's look at each other with a sense of compassion rather than jealousy. Let's offer our encouragement, not our envy.

Let's also begin to see one another as God sees us—beautifully made though imperfect people who are going through some of the same challenges. Let's begin to understand that our comparison is rooted in idealizing people rather than humanizing them.

I can assure you that the most "together" person you know suffers from comparison. The person you're measuring your life up against? She is measuring her life against someone else's . . . who is measuring hers against someone else's. And someone is comparing herself to you! It's a whole cycle of comparison that doesn't end unless some of us say enough is enough.

We could waste years wishing for something different—and then come across a photograph of ourselves twenty years later and realize that we walked right past the happy moments we were given.

The art of happy-making begins when we find our happiness within instead of without.

God chose us for this life of happiness in him. As Paul wrote, "Since this is the kind of life we have chosen, the life of the Spirit, let us make sure that we do not just hold it as an idea in our heads or a sentiment in our hearts, but work out its implications in every detail of our lives. That means we will not compare ourselves with each other as if one of us were better and another worse. We have far more interesting things to do with our lives."[8]

The Declaration of Good Enough

Let this be the declaration of those who will live by the Principle of Good Enough.

I am a person.

I am not a machine, a spreadsheet, an agenda, or a résumé.

I am a person.

I have a heartbeat, skin, scars, and soul.

I am a person.

My worth isn't calculated in efficiencies, results, boxes checked, or ladders climbed. I am not the sum of my accomplishments—or the sum of my mistakes. I am not my ambition, my energy level, my approval rating, my mass appeal, or my worth to the company store. I am not a stage or a platform or a gold star. I am not an A-plus or a D-minus. I am not a mess or a miscalculation.

I am not a mistake. I am a miracle.

Because I am a person, made of love and dirt in the hands of God.

I will be a person today. I will be me. I will resist the urge to believe that I've got to fight for my piece; God says there's more than enough to go around. I will take a leap into the pool of his grace; it's bottomless.

I will see the best in others and recognize the best in myself. I will believe that good enough is good enough, not only for myself, but also for other people.

I will reach for virtue more than trophies, dignity more than stardom. I will choose encouragement over envy. I will rejoice with those who rejoice.

I will live free and love well. I will stand tall on the inside, even if I'm feeling weak on the outside.

I am a person, a citizen of the Kingdom of God. I will live there as a Kingdom child. I will dwell where there is always enough, where there is abundant love, where there is unending grace for me.

Because I am a person, and I belong to Jesus.

Digging Deeper • • • • • • • • • • • • • • • • • •

1. *If I could just be like her.* How have you seen this Happiness Hijacker at work?

2. Is it easy for you to live by the Principle of Good Enough, or does that kind of principle make you feel like a slacker? Explain.

3. How can we enlarge our happiness by rejoicing with those who rejoice (Romans 12:15)? How can rejoicing with others reduce our urge to compare?

The Principle of Good Enough

1. **Be a "satisficer."**
   Let good enough be good enough with a
   task today.

2. **Congratulate someone.**
   Take five minutes to write a note applauding
   someone else instead of dwelling on the fact that
   she got what you wanted.

3. **Rejoice with those who rejoice.**
   Take a few minutes to pray and praise God for
   the accomplishments of others, including someone you've seen as a competitor.

4. **Journal for five minutes.**
   Use these words as a prompt: "I didn't ask you to
   be her. I asked you to be you."

5. **Acknowledge that others struggle with
   insecurity.**
   Go out of your way to send someone a text telling
   her what you see in her. You'll both feel happier!

6. **Take yourself less seriously.**
   Dedicate five minutes to play. Learn a joke, play
   Words with Friends, or sing a silly song.

7. **Make a commitment.**
   Write down one thing you would do if you
   weren't scared. Then make a plan to do it.

CHAPTER 13

The Principle of
Putting Up Your Dukes

❧

HAPPINESS HIJACKER:
My life circumstances make happiness an impossible dream.

HAPPINESS BOOSTER:
*I will muster up whatever happiness I do have
and wield it as a powerful weapon.*

And then I got sick.

Right in the middle of the Happiness Dare, I got as sick as I ever remember being.

Food repulsed me. I spent an unusual amount of time in the bathroom. Fatigue flattened me on the couch for days.

I was not okay.

I sat motionless in front of the fireplace. The clock moved its hands in a slow circle, and time felt heavy. The children would move quietly around me, whispering as if their words might break me in two. Scott would come in from farm chores, put a hand to my forehead, and bring me plates of crackers. Night after night, he sat in the leather recliner, Bible open, rubbing his creased forehead while praying for me to get better.

My body had surrendered under the sickness while we waited

for test results to come back. My happiness disappeared with my health, and I didn't know when I would find it again.

One day, I posted a picture of my sick self to my Facebook page. This was unlike me. I am not an oversharer and I restrain myself from making posts to social media that look like invitations for "sympathy likes." Maybe I was under the spell of fever-induced weakness. Maybe I had been lured in by my own chatter about risking vulnerability. I can't say for sure, but after finally being diagnosed with a severe intestinal infection, I posted a picture of sad, unwell me.

My brother told me I looked homeless, like someone who had found a quiet corner in an alley somewhere. I didn't care. I needed to let someone into my sad place.

I wrote this on Facebook:

> I have been feeling rather sorry for myself, unable
> to do a lot of the things I love to do, on account of
> being so ill. I was diagnosed with C. Diff on Friday.
> I couldn't join my family at church today. I don't have
> the energy to write on my blog. I've been too tired to
> put my own children to bed. I've spent approximately
> 72 percent of my waking hours in the bathroom.
> Food tastes horrible.
>
> But then, gospel happened. I "went" to church this
> morning online. (Isn't that something, how we can do
> that these days?) The gospel saved my sorry self again.
> The pastor—his name is Adam[1]—reminded me about
> the good in my life, even on the sick and sad days.
>
> See: I am down, but not defeated. I may *look*
> homeless, but I have a soft cushion under my head

and a roof over me and a family around me, praying.
I have Jesus.

I am not alone. And you, my friend, are not alone.
We are gonna make it. You know that? We really are.
This is not the end of the story. Not my illness, or
your heartbreak, or your missed flight, or the broken
relationships, or the lost job, or (_____). It is
not the end of the story. It is just a plot twist. The best
ending imaginable is coming. We are gonna make it.

We're going to be okay.

Right now, I'm not okay. But I'm going to be okay.

At the time, I needed to say all of that for my sake. But
maybe it's for you too. Because some of you are not okay right
now. And the rest of us? We may have hard days ahead. I don't
want to be a Debbie Downer, but the truth is that we all have
not-okay days. There is a 100 percent guarantee that trouble
will befall us during our time on earth. Jesus said, "In this world
you *will* have trouble."[2] There are simply going to be times of
misery in our lives.

I can't write a book about happiness without making space
for the very palpable reality of great unhappiness.

We have courageously taken the Happiness Dare. We've
believed what, perhaps, we never dared to believe before: that
our happiness matters to God. We now realize we have permission to be happy because that's a vital part of what it means to
be holy. We have learned how God uniquely wired us for happiness. And we have begun the spiritual practice of happiness by
dedicating at least five minutes a day to expanding our sweet
spots of happiness.

On the pages of this book, we've gone head-to-head with the myth that God doesn't care about our happiness. And we're not turning back now.

But you know what would be really awful? If you thought you didn't have permission to be sad anymore. Maybe you need to know this: You have permission to feel sorrow. It's okay to cry. The God who gave you your smile also gave you your tear ducts.

Let us draft a joint resolution that states the following: "We are hereby not okay sometimes. And that is okay."

The Ministry of Tears

A few nights ago, our family gathered to watch the Pixar animated movie *Inside Out* on DVD.

In the movie, viewers are taken inside the mind of a young girl named Riley. Inside of Riley's head, we meet the emotions influencing her: Joy, Sadness, Fear, Anger, and Disgust. All of the emotions are animated characters with their own sets of strengths and flaws. Joy, a lighthearted optimist, sees it as her personal mission to keep Riley happy, and she tries hard to prevent Sadness from gaining a foothold.

My favorite part of the movie happens when Joy has a startling revelation. She realizes that without Sadness, the little girl whom they inhabit would never have been able to navigate the hardest moments of her life. In that moment, Joy begins to weep.

This is what I know: Happiness weeps. Happiness knows the taste of salt in our tears.

Happiness—genuine happiness—allows space for a person

to be sad. No person who says she is happy can really be happy if she isn't ever sad. She can't ever be truly happy if she isn't given permission to be sad, if she doesn't have safe places to grieve, if she doesn't cry.

Happy people cry.

Happy people are familiar with the feel of thunderclouds building up on their insides. Happy people are the people who know it's a waste of effort to show up somewhere with the plastered-on Sunday smile.

Truly happy people are the ones who know what it feels like to be decidedly unjolly. They understand the ministry of a smile, but they also practice the ministry of tears. They have written sad poems and mournful songs for the rest of us when we need the words and the minor-key hymns to wrap around our own hurts. Legitimately happy people aren't afraid of our melancholic conversations, our cheerless days, or our Facebook posts when we look homeless.

Happy people are the ones who bring the Kleenex because they know that, while unhappiness doesn't last forever, it's a guaranteed part of life. The happiest people I know are the people who have gone through hard times and aren't afraid to sit down with someone else in their chaos.

Happy people don't turn away. They sit right in the middle of our mess with us and they cup the broken pieces in their hands as if to say, "Here, maybe I can help you with this." And then they lift those broken shards up to God on our behalf because we don't have the strength to do it on our own.

If you are crying today, that doesn't make you an unhappy person. It actually makes you more like Jesus. You know why?

Because real happiness can't happen apart from knowing

that Jesus wept.[3] Real happiness acknowledges that the same God who created the salt in your tears is the very God who bottles every one of them up.[4]

What a terrible thing it would be to demand that people be merry always. We would be robotic smile-slap-on-ers. We would offend the sensibilities of a hurting world.

This old world is a mix of the beautiful and the awful. We don't have to fear it.

The Bible reminds us that we do not grieve as those who have no hope. *But still, we grieve.* There are times ahead for all of us where misery and strife will overwhelm us. Or it might be dark now, but the light is up ahead. Take the time you need to reach the light. Walk slowly if you must. You get to pick the pace. Along the way, feel all of your feelings. This is you, getting in touch with your humanity.

So many people spend life running away from what makes them feel sad. They might numb their feelings with alcohol, retail therapy, or food. Doers might be tempted to get lost in their work as a way to mask the pain. Relaters might pin all their hopes on a relationship, making a friend or spouse their savior. Experiencers might be tempted to run from place to place in search of meaning. But no one will ever find real happiness if they feed their sad selves a meal of false happiness.

Feeling sad is a part of what makes your happiness more real and durable. After you have tasted gray, you no longer take for granted the feasts of yellow.

I am not interested in a kind of happiness that does not allow me to grieve or have hurt feelings when I have reasons for my feelings to be hurt. I cannot deal with a kind of happiness that denies my other real emotions.

Happiness doesn't deny our pain. It holds it gently. Happiness doesn't ignore the hurt of the world, but it makes a space to sit quietly inside of the ache.

I don't know what sadness you're facing and I have no way of knowing what's ahead for you—or for me. But I know that we have permission to feel it. We don't have to feel bad for feeling bad, even if someone else's "bad" is worse than ours.

People classify their sadness on some sort of invisible scale that is not at all helpful. When I was sick by the fire, for instance, I remember entertaining that kind of wrong thinking. I thought to myself, *I have no reason to be so sad! At least I have an actual diagnosis and at least it isn't terminal. I will get better. So I have no right to complain.*

That kind of attitude is decidedly unhelpful. Comparing sadness levels sanitizes our own sadness in such a way to deny us our humanity. It's a reverse form of happiness shaming.

When we acknowledge our own aches, only then can we fight for a way out of them.

The Fight for Happiness

We have to feel our feelings first, before we take another step toward recapturing the happiness we believe exists. There really is a way forward to happiness, you know.

The first step is dismantling one of the four statements we tell ourselves: *My life circumstances make happiness an impossible dream.*

Those words are standing in the way of a lot of happiness for many of us. Many people think that their happiness is irretrievably lost. Many people lose the will to fight for happiness when their worst nightmares come true. But we are not hopeless in our unhappiness. The happiness we once knew can be ours again, or perhaps we can discover it for the first time. When we fight for happiness, we aren't denying the pain of this world, but we are refusing to give in to it.

Begin by taking whatever shred of happiness you can muster up within you—and use it as a weapon.

A weapon?

Yes, you read that right.

Some see happiness as a weak, indulgent emotion. But God doesn't see it that way at all. He sees happiness as a strength, something that you can wield like a weapon.

It's right there in the Scriptures. Nehemiah said, "The joy of the LORD is your *strength*."[5]

Joy is strength. It has muscle. It's what can make you strong in this busted-up world of manifold heartbreak. When we are flattened under the curse of the world, joy is what will help us rise up again, fist in the air.

I know it's hard. It's easier to give in to the tidal wave of cynicism in our world. Choosing happiness is courageous. Happiness is the virtue of the brave, not the weak.

Happiness can be like venom to the enemy of your soul. You probably know from your high school health class that there's a chemical called *serotonin* inside of us. God gave us that chemical to help us experience feelings of happiness.

But maybe you didn't know this: You can leverage your serotonin as a weapon. That's what animals do. In some venomous animals, serotonin is a key ingredient in venom. The venom of some sea urchins, scorpions, spiders, and stingrays includes serotonin! The chemical that makes us feel happy is *the same chemical that works as a weapon.*[6]

You have that chemical in your own personal arsenal. Happiness is your venom against whatever tries to harm you. Happiness is a weapon against your prowling enemy.

This is why I am committed to devoting five minutes or more every day to happiness. It's a way to fight back against the rancor of the world. It's the reason so many of us make gratitude lists. We have to retrain our brains to counteract our tendency toward negativity.

I've had to use happiness as a weapon when the pain cut so deep it hurt my insides. I've used happiness as a weapon during anxiety attacks and bouts of depression and illness. I've had to wield happiness like a sword after deep grief enveloped the whole of me. Like you, I've stood on the cruel edge of earth, waiting for the casket to be lowered.

Happiness didn't come in the middle of my grief. We all have to allow ourselves to feel sorrow, sometimes for long seasons. But there always comes a time when we are summoned to rise up again, sword in hand. This is what will save us.

But maybe you're thinking to yourself, *Well, you haven't dealt with what I have, Jennifer. You don't know how hard it's been. You were able to stand back up again, but I never will be.*

In one respect, you're right: I don't know what you've gone through. And because of that, I almost didn't write this book. How could I, for instance, tell you to choose happiness if you were diagnosed with a terminal illness yesterday? How could I have any credibility with a missionary from the developing world who hears the knuckled rap of unhappiness when a hungry child knocks on her door? How could I tell a woman to choose happiness after she has picked out a casket for her little girl? Does happiness work as a weapon then?

Here is my worst nightmare: death cruelly snatching one of the children whom God has placed in my care. That's the kind of nightmare that leaves me wondering how I could ever be happy again. I have recovered from other kinds of sadness. I have been wounded by the brokenness in this world, but I have eventually regained happiness by stretching toward that patch of hopeful light resting beyond the dark corner where I've cowered.

In the middle of my Happiness Dare, I had to know: Can a woman find happiness if she's lived my worst nightmare?

I sat at a table with another Jennifer to find out. She might be the bravest woman I've ever met.

The Woman Who Made Happiness a Weapon

I met with Jennifer on an October night at a coffee shop in northwest Iowa as the trees began to blush, their leaves drifting to the ground. She told me about her three-year-old daughter, Autumn.

"She was so full of life, so affectionate, and she gave the tightest hugs to anyone who asked for one," Jennifer told me. Autumn loved to ride her tricycle, watch *Dora the Explorer*, and play dress up. She loved "Jesus music" and had mastered the art of the rock-star fist.

In 2013, a call came from Autumn's day-care provider. The day-care provider said Autumn had fallen down the stairs. Over the next several minutes, the situation grew progressively worse. Jennifer called her husband, instructing him to meet her at the hospital. Then she picked up Autumn at the day-care provider's home and rushed her to the emergency room.

A CT scan revealed a severe skull fracture.

I didn't know Jennifer when this happened. But that same day, my Facebook news feed was filled with links to Autumn's page on CaringBridge. I clicked a link and entered—as much as a stranger can—into the sorrow of another mom named Jennifer. Like thousands of others, I prayed. I believed God would heal that little girl.

Within a day, Autumn became more than the motivation of our prayers. She became a headline. Authorities said Autumn didn't fall down the stairs as her day-care provider had first reported. The injuries, investigators said, were caused by the day-care provider.[7]

Two days later, Jennifer sat at a computer keyboard in a hospital waiting room and wrote these words on her daughter's CaringBridge page:

> Phil and I met with the doctor in charge of Autumn's care a short while ago. The medical indicators show that the extent of her injuries is not compatible with life and she is, in essence, brain-dead. We have made the decision to stop all treatment. . . . We are not going to be selfish and continue to put her little body through things that are not doing any good. We believe our Lord is a healer and this time He has chosen to heal our little girl on His side of things—in heaven. . . .
>
> The 1st catechism question asks: What is your only comfort in life and in death? The answer to that question is: That I am not my own, but belong, body and soul, in life and in death, to my faithful Savior, Jesus Christ.

After Jennifer clicked Publish, Jennifer and Phil climbed into bed with their girl. Autumn's mama lay to her right, and her daddy lay to her left. The nurses unplugged each machine, one by one, and wheeled them out. All the while, Autumn's mom and dad sang over her. They sang all of her favorite Bible songs. And the whole time, that mama put a hand on her baby girl's heart.

At 5:40 p.m., Autumn's heart stopped. "We sang her over to the other side," Jennifer told me. "It's a really weird feeling, leaving the hospital one kid short."

I cannot fathom the depth of such grief. I cannot imagine how a mother could carry on, how she could ever feel happiness again, how she could ever feel human.

Jennifer wondered too. Despair swallowed her. She felt the words of the psalmist at her own core: "Darkness is my closest friend."[8]

"I pulled back from my friends and my husband. I went through a very dark period, thinking that if God can take Autumn away, he can take anything away," Jennifer said.

It was at her lowest that Jennifer learned how her own fight for happiness was a way out of her despair. Some of the most stunning journeys toward happiness begin in the darkest dark. And the candle that lights the way out is this tiny, flickering flame of hope.

"I had to move from darkness to light. I *had* to," Jennifer told me. "I had a husband. I had two other beautiful kids who were living and who needed me. I realized more than ever before how short our time is."

On Monday, July 14, 2014, Autumn would have turned four. That day, Jennifer took one small step out of the darkness—

applying the Principle of Small Daily Gains. She ordered a huge bouncy house, had pizzas delivered, and invited all of Autumn's friends over.

That courageous mama threw a party.

It didn't end there. She went onto her daughter's CaringBridge page and wrote these words.

> I have gone through a period of great darkness in my life, and it has been easier for me to live in my darkness rather than face the light that comes with being truthful. That will come as a surprise to some of you who know me . . . because I've become a master at putting on a happy face and laughing at the appropriate times. However, inside I've slowly been dying. I have pushed people away, I have lied, and I have fallen from the close relationship I used to have with God. However, I will not pull away from God any longer. He understands me better than anyone. I lost sight of that and am so thankful for those who have seen my darkness and are guiding me back into the light. Living in the light can be hard, especially when things you want to keep hidden need to be revealed, but it is the best place to be.

Then she asked for people to help her celebrate Autumn's birthday by bringing happiness to someone else—the hallmark act of Givers. Jennifer was making a life-changing discovery: Fighting for happiness is the way toward happiness. Happiness doesn't just happen. It's a choice we make every day.

That truth fluttered down and landed somewhere soft inside

of Jennifer when she put out the call to her CaringBridge readers. She wrote this:

> Make tomorrow special for someone else in Autumn's memory. Maybe you can call up that friend or family member you haven't spoken to in a while, pay for someone's meal or groceries, mow your neighbor's lawn, send your best friend flowers, visit someone living in a nursing home, bring your boss or day-care provider coffee or donuts, send someone a card. It is truly better to give than to receive, and I have found no greater joy than the joy I have found in doing something for someone else.

Jennifer's joy was discovered in creating joy for others. She took one small step out of the darkness and found a patch of light. Her call for random acts of kindness has grown into an annual event called Action for Autumn. It's held every year on Autumn's birthday. And now a center for children who have experienced abuse, grief, or neglect bears Autumn's name.

"I'll never forgot how, on that first birthday without Autumn, those small acts of giving made a very unbearable day bearable," Jennifer said.

Jennifer's fight for happiness doesn't deny the profound sadness she feels. Her deepest ache has not been eradicated. The emptiness in her heart can feel like a canyon.

"Autumn is never out of my thoughts," Jennifer says. All of life, she told me, is now imbued with more meaning. She feels everything deeper—both the sorrow and the joy. Every vacation. Every new day. Every baptism. Every Lord's Supper.

Every falling leaf of autumn. It all bears witness to the pain of her own great loss, alongside the glorious riches of the life she's still living with people she loves. Jennifer has known no greater sorrow, nor has she felt gratitude more deeply.

Every happy moment means more because she knows how fragile this life is.

Flex Your Happy

Ever since I met Jennifer, I have thought about how much we need the voices of people like her who have suffered deeply, for they show us the durability of our faith in the most unimaginable circumstances.

When I think of Jennifer, I think of Jesus, who demonstrated the comingling of joy and sadness. Happiness and sorrow dwelt simultaneously inside of our Savior.

On the night he was betrayed, Jesus told his disciples to abide in him and hold fast to his teachings. He told them to remain in his love and obey even when it was hard.

"I have told you this to make you as completely happy as I am,"[9] Jesus said.

Jesus was most certainly a "man of sorrows," yet he willingly went to the cross "for the *joy* set before him."[10]

Not for the duty set before him. Not for the obligation set before him.

For the joy.

Astounding.

Jesus gives us that same power—to move forward with joy, even on the hardest days. Jesus gave us everything we need to fight back against the tide of negativity by giving us the Holy

Spirit and the fruit borne from a life lived in the Spirit. We have happiness built inside us, and we can flex it like a muscle. With practice and commitment, we can also strengthen that muscle. That's what it means to "flex your happy."

When I was a little girl, I loved the phrase "put up your dukes." I suppose that's because I was a scrawny little Dukes girl, and it astounded me that such a powerful phrase could include my last name. I viewed myself as small, weak, incapable at times, unsure of myself in times of trial. The phrase felt empowering.

There are several theories about how the phrase "put up your dukes" came into use.

My favorite theory suggests that "put up your dukes" referred to a king summoning his dukes, knights, and soldiers into battle against an enemy. As a follower of King Jesus, I love that image.

Maybe all of us are dukes. And we have a King calling us into battle against a real enemy. The King is "putting up his dukes," and that means he's putting up us. We are the dukes, no matter how weak and incapable we feel today.

He is summoning us. And when we're ready to heed his call, we can practice the Principle of Putting Up Your Dukes. We can fight for happiness and wield it like a weapon. We can flex our happy. No matter what we're facing, we get to choose how we'll fight.

Here is the surprising secret to happiness that we all need to know: The way to happiness is happiness itself. The way to find happiness is to fight for it.

Maybe you're not ready to fight yet. That's okay. Go easy on yourself. Maybe you're like my friend Beth, a woman who has endured great pain in her life the last three years. Sometimes, she told me, fighting for happiness sounds like a lot of work: "My first thought is that happiness is a three-syllable word, and some days that just feels like too much. It's hard to live, and it's too big of a word to say."

Some days you're not ready for a three-syllable word. Some days you're not ready for a fight. Be still. Breathe. Remember: It's okay to not be okay.

But there will come a day when you know that the fight is what will save you. The fight is in you because Jesus is in you. Christ in you, the hope of glory. The hope of everything.

Digging Deeper • • • • • • • • • • • • • • •

1. *My life circumstances make happiness an impossible dream.* How have you seen this Happiness Hijacker at work?

2. Jennifer says we should draft a joint resolution that states the following: "We are hereby not okay sometimes. And that is okay." Do you agree? Should there be a statute of limitations on being "not okay"? Why or why not?

3. How can feeling sad make a person's happiness more real, durable, and sustaining in the long run?

4. How can you "flex your happy" on a hard day? Or does that seem unrealistic to you right now?

Five-Minute Happiness Hacks

The Principle of Putting Up Your Dukes

1. **Perform a random act of kindness.**
   Pick a random act of kindness from the list Autumn's mom created. (See page 238.)

2. **Send a happy greeting.**
   Send one card to someone every day for the next week. (My brother-in-law Mike has done this for four years. He sends two cards a day to anyone needing encouragement or simply to congratulate others on a job well done. "It makes me happy to make someone else's day," Mike says.)

3. **Practice the ministry of the smile.**
   Smile at friends, family members, and strangers in the store. Studies show smiling is contagious.

4. **Practice the ministry of tears.**
   Let yourself cry when you must. And allow yourself to weep with those who weep.

5. **Take the offer of help.**
   When someone offers to help you when you're down, let her. It brings that person joy to be there for you, and it will bring you needed relief.

6. **Tell someone how you feel.**
   One Swedish proverb says, "Shared joy is a double joy; shared sorrow is half a sorrow." Share your joy or sorrow with someone else.

CHAPTER 14

The Principle of the Head-to-Foot Alleluia

~⟨~

HAPPINESS HIJACKER:
If only I had (_____).

HAPPINESS BOOSTER:
*I will be grateful for what already is
instead of wishing for what could be.*

It was the week before Thanksgiving. Outside my kitchen window, it looked more like Christmas, like maybe we'd been set inside a real-life snow globe.

A record-breaking seventeen inches of snow fell the day before. When I awoke that morning, just after dawn, it looked as if the earth had pulled a white duvet tight over its whole self, then drifted off for a long winter's nap.

I stood at the kitchen window, a spot where I can see for miles. I took it all in. I uttered a quiet thanks to God, in awe of the beauty he habitually creates. Gratitude seemed like the proper response, even knowing what was happening out beyond the borders of our magical snow globe.

Somewhere out there the wounded world was breaking again.

I could hear the newscaster on the television in the living room. The day's stories sounded like yesterday's stories: bloodshed, suicide bombers, attacks, high alerts.

Still, I said it again louder: "Thank you, Lord." Gratitude was more than a nice gesture acknowledging the sweet gift of an early snow. It was the stubborn refusal to be held hostage by fear and despair. It was, as G. K. Chesterton once noted, recognizing that "gratitude is happiness doubled by wonder." Because despite everything, this old world is still a beautiful place. No matter how hopeless it all seems, there's always, always something to be thankful for. We can be grateful in times of hopelessness because we are gripped at all times by God.

Cicero said that gratitude is not only the greatest of virtues, but the parent of all others. If that's true, then my happiness does not cause me to be grateful for what I have. My gratitude for what I have causes me to be happy. Gratitude births the virtue of happiness.

At the window, I chose gratitude.

Outside, a hushed beauty persisted. The ground sparkled, like God had embedded diamonds in the snow. The evergreens were flocked so heavily in white that they drooped under the weight. A thin pink line was drawn onto that place where the sky bent down to kiss the earth.

What a shame it would be if God created all of this and we didn't stop to notice. Even the coldest days of our lives can't be robbed of their inherent beauty because God is still in the business of giving good gifts.

I snapped a photo of the dawning on my smartphone—the light overtaking the dark, itself a miracle. This was my way of being intentional, of starting my day with thanks. It was a way of paying attention.

In my own Happiness Dare, I have hereby boycotted cynicism. I am determined to find the stubborn beauty in this busted-up world because I know the world-changing power of my own happiness. Happiness is more than a sappy feeling; it's the outward expression of the inward joy we have in Jesus. One of the best ways to hold on to your happiness in hard times is simply by saying thanks.

I have learned four things about the power of gratitude, the parent of happiness:

- On your best day, gratitude reminds you that your gifts are not your own. And on your worst day, gratitude reminds you that you are not alone.
- Gratitude is acknowledging the goodness in our lives as life exists today, not as we wish it to be.
- It's impossible for us to be happy and ungrateful at the same time.
- Gratitude is the strong foundation on which our ultimate happiness is built.

The Flaw of "If Only" Thinking

One of the four major obstacles standing in the way of happiness is the belief that we would be happy "if only. . . ." We miss out on a fuller, richer happiness when we wish for what could be while neglecting to be grateful for what already is.

Our happiness gets held hostage by a long line of if-onlys.

One of the best
ways to hold on
to your happiness
in hard times is
simply by saying,
"Thanks."

"If only we could have peace in this conflicted world."

"If only winter wasn't so cold."

"If only summer wasn't so hot."

When the kids are toddlers, we say, "If only the kids were older."

And when they turn into teenagers with raging hormones, we hear ourselves saying, "If only they were little again."

There are lesser if-onlys, but they serve as bandits of happiness regardless:

"If only I had her abs."

"If only my boss wasn't such a jerk."

"If only I could catch a break."

The plague of "if only" doesn't fall too far from our ancestral apple tree. Our spiritual ancestors, the Israelites, had been freed from slavery but found themselves unhappily wandering in the wilderness. God faithfully provided nourishment for the journey—heaven-made sack lunches—by miraculously dropping food from the sky.

Imagine the happiness they felt when the first food appeared on the ground. A psalmist later referred to the manna as the "bread of angels."[1] Before long, though, familiarity bred contempt. They grew tired of the same old meal day after day. They longingly remembered the fish, cucumbers, melons, and leeks that they had eaten back in Egypt. They were soon plagued by their own if-onlys.

"If only we had meat to eat!"[2]

It got more dire: "If only we had died in Egypt!"[3]

Like the Israelites, we grow tired of our lots and bank our happiness on if-onlys.

If-only happiness is happiness deferred. It postpones happiness for another place and another time.

We might be tempted to think that we'll find greatest happiness in the Bahamas, but do we not see the beauty under our feet, whether we're in Fargo or Phoenix or Fearnot, Pennsylvania?

When we took the Happiness Dare, we surrendered ourselves to the promise that God has given us everything we need to find happiness in the here and now, regardless of circumstances. We also came to understand that he equipped us to uniquely experience happiness in the world as Doers, Relaters, Experiencers, Givers, and Thinkers.

No matter what our style, the richest form of happiness begins with two words: "Thank you." It begins by recognizing the gifts we've already been given and taking the time to be grateful for them. The answer to the myth of "if only" is the Principle of the Head-to-Foot Alleluia.

It was Augustine who said it first: "A Christian should be an Alleluia from head to foot." Not waist to foot. Not armpit to foot. But head to foot. If gratitude is directly proportional to my happiness, I will be far happier on the days when I am grateful from scalp to toes.

All human beings—no matter what they believe about God—have the built-in potential to experience profound gratitude. Secular research consistently points to thankfulness as a foundational piece of happiness. But imagine what it would be like if you had to direct all of your thankfulness to fate or to the thin air or to your "lucky stars." Without God, you have nowhere in particular to guide your gratitude.

But if we know God, we have a tremendous advantage when

it comes to gratitude and happiness: We know where to direct our thanks. If we belong to Jesus, we have the ultimate reason to live the Principle of the Head-to-Foot Alleluia. We don't have to be held hostage by our long lists of if-onlys anymore.

We can be grateful for life as it exists today, not as we wish it to be.

The Story of a Grateful Woman

I don't believe in Pollyanna answers. Neither do you. We need to know that gratitude-based happiness really works. Corrie ten Boom shows us how.

Corrie ten Boom was a Dutch Christian who was imprisoned for helping Jews escape the Holocaust. She was the kind of woman who practiced radical gratitude and understood genuine happiness. "Happiness," she once said, "isn't something that depends on our surroundings. It's something we make inside ourselves."

Corrie ten Boom lived the Principle of the Head-to-Foot Alleluia. She told a remarkable tale of gratitude in her classic book *The Hiding Place*. The book tells of her imprisonment in a concentration camp with her sister Betsie. They had been assigned to sleep in a filthy barracks where the plumbing had backed up. They slept on straw-covered platforms, while nausea swept over them from the awful stench. Fleas began to swarm around them.

"How can we live in this place?" Corrie asked her sister.

Betsie prayed to God: "Show us how."

This is what happened next, in an exchange between the two sisters:

"Corrie!" she [Betsie] said excitedly. . . . "In the Bible this morning. Where was it? Read that part again!"

I glanced down the long dim aisle to make sure no guard was in sight, then drew the Bible from its pouch. "It was in First Thessalonians," I said. . . .

"Oh yes: '. . . to one another and to all. Rejoice always, pray constantly, give thanks in all circumstances—'"

"That's it, Corrie! That's His answer. 'Give thanks in all circumstances!' That's what we can do."[4]

The two women then made a mental gratitude list in the foul-aired room where they lay. The list included being assigned together, rather than separately; the fact that they were able to sneak their Bible past the inspectors; the crammed room, which meant that more ears would hear the gospel.

In the nights to come, the sisters would hold worship services in the rear of the dormitory room under a single lightbulb.[5] Then they took the message of the gospel to their work centers at the camp.

"Thus began the closest, most joyous weeks of all the time in Ravensbruck. . . . In the sanctuary of God's fleas, Betsie and I ministered the Word of God to all in the room. We sat by deathbeds that became doorways of heaven. We watched women who had lost everything grow rich in hope. . . . We prayed beyond the concrete walls for the healing of Germany, of Europe, of the world."[6]

From the seed of gratitude was born an inner happiness that helped Corrie cope, while giving her a rich vision of carrying her hope to the world.

A Lesson from a Lone Leper

Gulp. So yeah. That's a little convicting, isn't it?

When I first read how Corrie ten Boom practiced radical gratitude in a flea-infested death camp, I thought about how often I have failed the gratitude test.

I have been lulled into unhappiness under the weight of far lesser challenges. I've felt burned out and unhappy in a comfortable office cubicle, when I could have felt grateful that I had a job. I have been decidedly grumpy while scrubbing a ring from a bathtub, instead of expressing thanks that I had running water. God knows I've whined while dealing with yet another case of adult acne.

And here we meet Corrie and Betsie, thanking God in a "sanctuary of God's fleas."

Corrie's story isn't in this book to shame us toward gratitude. It's in this book to show us the power of stubborn thanks, the refusal to let the world drag us down.

The truth is, most of us have no idea what it feels like to live imprisoned, fearful for our lives. Most of us have full refrigerators, closets with clothes, garages with cars, and cars with gas. We have a lot of stuff that's supposed to make us happy, but oddly, we still sink into feelings of ungratefulness. (That's a clue that happiness has less to do with how much we have and everything to do with how grateful we are.)

Stories like Corrie's remind us that happiness is possible outside of circumstances and inside of Christ. Stories like hers show us that the people who fight for happiness aren't frail-minded people. They are the strong ones. They are the ones who hold church under a single lightbulb in a concentration camp. They are the ones who sit in hospital rooms next to loved ones while making lists in their gratitude journals. They know that all of this, all of life, is a gift and that they walk only in the strength of Jesus. They press on in his love, grateful that it always covers us.

They are also the ones who pause to give thanks on their very best days. They remember the source of all good gifts. They stop to say thanks when the unlikely cure happens, when the money miraculously appears, when they fall madly in love, when the whole family comes home for Thanksgiving. The grateful people acknowledge the good in their lives and they remember who gave it in the first place.

Will we be the lone leper who comes back to thank Jesus?

Jesus healed ten people in all. How happy all ten of them must have been to receive a miraculous cure. Imagine the relief. Imagine how they compared notes of their healing. Imagine the excited pitches of their voices, their eyes widening from the wonder at what had just happened.

Imagine the happiness!

Imagine the spring in their steps as they skipped away from their healer, eager to live a new life. And skip away they did. Nine of them walked on, backs to Jesus, without so much as a thank you.

All but one.

In his Gospel, Luke recounts: "One of them, when he saw that he was healed, turned back, praising God with a loud voice; and he fell on his face at Jesus' feet, giving him thanks."

Jesus then asked the healed man two questions. Imagine the look in Jesus' eyes when he asked: "Were not ten cleansed? Where are the nine?" Jesus then gave the lone leper a spiritual healing that far exceeded the gift of physical healing: "Rise and go your way; your faith has made you well."[7]

All ten lepers had reason to be happy. But only the one who offered gratitude experienced a more potent kind of happiness. All because he turned around. All because he said thank you.

His greatest happiness came *as a direct result* of his heartfelt gratitude.

Think of gratitude-based happiness as multiplied happiness. When we stop to say thank you, we bring delight to the Giver. Furthermore, we are given an extra happiness tied directly to our gratitude.

Our thankfulness is more than the polite response for a gift. It's the heart-moving response that stretches all the way to the Giver.

The Art of Paying Attention

Once again, science has caught up with what God has been saying all along.

Volumes of research have linked gratitude to happiness. Daily efforts at keeping a positive focus are associated with more alertness, attentiveness, and altruism. And that's just the *A*'s. People who are grateful are more optimistic, motivated, forgiving, helpful, healthy, and likely to give back to their communities.

In one study, researchers divided participants into groups. One group was told to take note of everything they were grateful for. Another group was told to write about the daily irritations and annoyances of life.

Here's what both groups had in common: Both were asked to pay attention.

After ten weeks, the people who wrote about gratitude had a more optimistic outlook on their lives. They also exercised more and had fewer doctors' visits than those who wrote about their negative experiences.[8]

What they paid attention to affected their happiness. When we reflect on the good in our lives, we experience residual happiness. And when we record the good of the past, our brains learn to scan for the good in the future. Our brains begin to look forward in expectancy—offering a boost of anticipatory happiness.

It's all about paying attention.

Researcher Shawn Achor says that when you write even a short list of three good things that happened in a day, your brain is forced to scan the last twenty-four-hour period to rediscover all the things that made you smile and gave you hope.[9]

When we look for things that make us grateful, we start seeing them. And when we start noticing them, we are making actual investments in the thoughts of our future selves. We are building neural pathways, all the while becoming more resourced on the inside. When we are more resourced with happiness, we have a kind of happiness bank that we can draw from on our hardest days.

We can begin accumulating resources in our happiness banks by taking five minutes every day to consider our blessings. It's a good practice to write them down, but you don't have to. Merely *thinking* of your blessings has a profound effect on your outlook. We can devote five minutes a day, dwelling on the good things and thanking the one who gave them to us. I understand that you may not be one of those unstoppably positive people whom you know—the kind of person who wakes up singing songs, the kind of person who relentlessly posts cuddly puppy pictures on Facebook. I understand how you might be inclined to forgo counting your blessings on your hardest days. And I totally get how it feels selfish to make a list of what's right in your little world when you know there's a girl in a developing country who can see the ribs under her skin.

Thank God anyway. We must.

As Ann Voskamp writes, "I only deepen the wound of the world when I neglect to give thanks for early light dappled through leaves and the heavy perfume of wild roses in early July and the song of crickets on humid nights and the rivers that run and the stars that rise and the rain that falls and all the good things that a good God gives."[10]

There are so many good gifts here in this world. Clean sheets and Frisbee golf and kites and reruns of *Friends*. A cool breeze through a cracked window. *A Charlie Brown Christmas* on a cold December night. An overdue date with your husband, and his arm over your shoulder at the movies. A new bottle of bubble bath, a fresh haircut, leggings-and-boots weather, the smell of a bookstore, a long rope of licorice.

Thank God for what you have been given and then use your gratefulness as a way to share the gospel with a world in need of a reason to praise.

Furthermore, you can use your gratefulness as fuel to nourish your own happiness style. Maybe it could look a little bit like this:

Doers: Pray for the customer at your store, the reader of your latest blog post, the hospital patient you are

tending to tomorrow. Be thankful that you've been
given the opportunity to serve them—and the privilege
to pray for them.

Relaters: Don't wait until it's too late to tell someone how
much they mean to you. Don't wait until it's too late to
say, simply, "I love you."

Experiencers: Be grateful that God has given you this
wild and wonderful world to enjoy. Let your gratitude
overflow so much that you can't keep it to yourself:
invite a friend into your next big adventure.

Givers: Sponsor the girl who can see her ribs, deliver
blankets to the homeless vets in your town, sign up for
the Big Sisters program, invite the neighbor to church.
Practice gratitude by being thankful for your resources,
which you use to help others.

Thinkers: Thank the good Lord above for your
ridiculously beautiful mind. But by all means, don't
keep it to yourself! Use that mind to solve a problem
or ask a question that no one else has dared to ask.

Look: Anyone can be a cynic. Anyone can withhold thanks
and hold grudges and come up with a thousand reasons to be
unhappy today. It takes a strong person to look for the light. It
takes a strong person to wield gratitude like a weapon. It takes
a strong person to seek crazy-hard for the good and to insist on
seeing the glass as half-full.

Over the last few years, our family has taken several trips to
Haiti, often staying at an orphanage across the bay from Port-
au-Prince. The children show us what it looks like to live out
the Principle of the Head-to-Foot Alleluia.

Every night, after dinner, the children lead their friends in prayer. Together they face each of the four walls of the orphanage and shout, *"Le san de Jezi!"* They are praying the words *The blood of Jesus* to the north, south, east, and west. Afterward, they break out in songs of praise and thanksgiving.

Maybe somewhere deep inside them, they are thinking what any of us would naturally think in their circumstances:

I would be happier, if only I had parents.

If only I lived in a safer country.

If only I could be assured a job when I grow up.

If only people outside these walls weren't dying.

But instead of ending their days with if-onlys, they end their days with the head-to-foot alleluia. *Their gratitude is contagious.*

After witnessing this moving display of gratitude on a recent visit, we watched the following morning as a four-year-old girl named Nadege instructed her toddler friends to sit down on the bench, just like she'd seen the older kids do the night before. Then Nadege—who'd come to that orphanage terribly malnourished a few months earlier—stood up in front of them like a tiny preacher. She tossed back her head, lifting her face to the sky, and stretched out both arms to heaven, shouting, "Alleluia!"

And you know what? Nadege's gratitude was contagious.

Because this is what happened next: The young children did exactly what Nadege did. They shouted "Alleluia! Alleluia!" over and over again. When Nadege danced in a circle, the children danced in circles. When she shouted alleluia, they did the same.

And you know what else? The toddlers' gratitude was contagious too.

One morning, just after the roosters began to crow, I sat on the deck, watching the sun rise over the bay. In the room below, I heard tiny voices in a growing chorus. It was the "baby room," where the littlest children of the orphanage sleep. The children had begun to wake up, and they wanted someone to come and get them out of their cribs.

But they didn't whimper or wail.

They didn't say, "Mama, come get me!"

At first I couldn't make out what they were saying, but when I opened the door, I heard it clear as day. They were shouting this one word, again and again: "Alleluia! Alleluia!"

I began to weep tears of happiness, of gratitude, of the contagious alleluia. Here were all these boys—maybe one or two years old—gripping the edges of their cribs, shouting their thanks.

Maybe this is what we could all do every day. It's at least a good place to start, to live our lives in this repeat cycle of waking up with the alleluia on our lips. We could cry out for God to come and get us; we could shout our alleluia. And all day long, we could sing it—with Nadege and the babies—our continual thanksgiving to the heavens. And then, as night falls, we could face north, south, east, and west and pray the blood of Jesus over it all.

Maybe you've met happy people like that. Maybe you've met them in Haiti or along the red-dirt roads of Uganda—where there are often few reasons other than God for people to be happy.

But maybe you've never had to cross an ocean. Maybe you see the happiest people right where you are—in the Deep South, or on the snow-covered plains of North Dakota, or in the soft chairs of your living room. I hope you see them in your carpool lane, on your cul-de-sac. I hope you see them in your own mirror.

Let's be those people, the ones who make people talk because they hear us shouting alleluia. We are the dare takers who, like Flannery O'Connor, are "stalking joy—fully armed too as it's a highly dangerous quest."

Believe me, I know that there are days when happiness seems like an awful lot of work. You get the cold shoulder, the rejection letter, the unwanted call from the doctor. Your beloved pet dies, your child is bullied, and nothing you say seems to matter to your kid. You want to bury your head in the pillow and close all the blinds, forever and ever, amen.

But those are the days when happiness is *absolutely worth the work*—even if it's hard. Because sometimes happiness is what will save us. Those small glimmers of hopefulness shimmer on the surface and let us know God hasn't left us here alone. Behold the beauty of small things: the gilded leaf, the sun sliding down the sky like an egg yolk, the way your hand has fit inside of his for all these years. Think on these things—the things that are true, noble, right, pure, and lovely. And thank God for them all. For they are everywhere, even in the unexpected places.

Have you seen the happy things, even in the NICU, in the waiting room, in the grocery aisle, wherever you are today? You may have to look really, really hard, but looking is what changes things. The looking is the decision that flips the switch somewhere inside of us. The looking is what makes us brave in a world that says, "There's nothing good to see here anymore."

On the hardest days, I wish that happiness arrived in a box, like a pizza at the door. But happiness isn't a pizza. Sometimes it's a choice. It doesn't just happen. It's a decision we make every day.

When we find it—and we will find it—we won't skip away. We won't forget to turn around, even if everyone else keeps moving on, never looking back again. We won't forget to run back to Jesus and fall before him—like the lone leper—to offer all of our gratitude to him, the one who saved us and who is the reason for every alleluia, from head to foot.

Digging Deeper •••••••••••••••

1. *If only I had* _____ . How have you seen this Happiness Hijacker at work?

2. Study after study suggests that gratitude increases happiness. Based on your own life experience, how have you seen that to be true?

3. How can you be like the lone leper today? For what three things can you thank Jesus?

Five-Minute Happiness Hacks

The Principle of the Head-to-Foot Alleluia

1. **Practice the art of paying attention.**
   Write down three things a day that you're grateful for.

2. **Thank someone.**
   Write a letter of gratitude to someone who has influenced your life greatly.

3. **Share your happiness.**
   Snap photos of whatever makes you grateful and upload the photos to Instagram and Facebook with the hashtag #TheHappinessDare.

4. **Read *The Hiding Place* by Corrie ten Boom.**
   Five minutes a day, read this book and remind yourself that people can find reasons to be grateful in the most unlikely places.

5. **Spy little miracles everywhere.**
   Pray for God to expand your sense of wonder.

6. **Wake with the word *alleluia* on your lips.**
   Like the children at the Haitian orphanage, let *alleluia* be the first thing out of your mouth every morning.

7. **Be like the lone leper.**
   Take five minutes to turn around and thank Jesus. Then give him five minutes more.

CHAPTER 15

The Happiness Cycle

༥

When large numbers of people share their joy in common, the happiness of
each is greater because each adds fuel to the other's flame.
AUGUSTINE

We drove into town to help celebrate the first birthday of a boy
named John Dudley. We call him the *Dud-Man* for short.

This little guy is proof that God is in the business of pre-
meditated cuteness—the kind of cuteness that inspires embarrassing acts of adult aggression like the pinching and squeezing
of baby cheeks.[1]

Oh, that Dud-Man.

John Dudley is the firstborn son of some dear family friends,
and we were so excited to help him celebrate his first birthday.

After the birthday boy opened presents, his mom put him
in his high chair. A whole crowd of us gathered around. It was
the moment we'd all been waiting for. His mother had ordered
a personal-size round birthday cake, decorated with blue and
white frosting.

That cake was all his.

For quite a while, the cake sat in front of him, untouched. We all cheered John Dudley on, encouraging him, with raised eyebrows and high-pitched voices, to *go on now, dig in, honey; it's all yours!*

He scanned the crowd, left to right, as if to say: "Are Mom and Dad really going to let me eat *that*?"

At last, John Dudley stuck one tentative finger into the cake, pulled it out, and put a dollop of frosting into his mouth. It was his first glorious taste of the goodness that had been set before him.

His eyes grew big, like he'd been shocked by sweetness.

All of us laughed, and then we encouraged him to try some more. Which he did, with increasing enthusiasm and a growing trust that the cake before him was a gift to be enjoyed.

He had permission.

Soon, he shoved his tiny fists into the cake, scooping up huge gobs, making a general mess of his barely there hair, his bib, and those super-squeezable cheeks. Frosting fell below to a circling, hopeful dog. All of it was a portrait of happiness and innocence.

The crowd began to erupt with cheers and the flashing of cameras.

After a minute, I moved away from the crowd and circled around to stand behind the birthday boy's high chair near his grandpa.

"He's really something, isn't he?" Grandpa said proudly, with one of those big smiles that moves way up into a person's eyes.

"He sure is," I said, nodding.

And then I turned to see what Grandpa was seeing. From his

new vantage point, a beautiful picture emerged. I wondered if this is what God sees when his children are riveted by a moment of pure happiness.

Here's what I saw: happy parents, aunts and uncles, cousins and neighbors, and friends, all enraptured by a happy boy enjoying his cake. They held up their smartphones to get good pictures. They threw back their heads with laughter and they leaned in closer for a better look. Every eye was trained on the boy.

Someone so small offered so much to so many.

Standing there in that moment, I thought of you, the dare takers.

God has set a cake before you. It was made especially for you because he loves you. No one has ever been given a cake quite like yours. You might still be looking around, unsure if you should dig in. What if you don't have permission? What if you make a mess? What if there's not enough for everyone else?

Friend, the cake is yours.

And guess what? I have one too. I have a cake just for me. It's perfect. It has blue frosting. And it's decorated with little yellow candies that are laid out to spell the word *happiness*. Long ropes of licorice are looped to spell the word *dare*. There are gumdrops and peppermints too.

I hear there's enough for everyone. We all have a cake!

Somewhere out there, right now, somebody is already enjoying her cake. And if she's lucky, she's got a tribe of people who don't envy her moment in the spotlight but instead take delight in *her* delight. They aren't wishing it were theirs. They don't believe the lies about scarcity. They are present-tense, fully engaged, wide-eyed with wonder—celebrating the joy that someone else is experiencing.

There is no envy there—only happiness.

And then look further back. Look outside the main frame. There stands another figure, like an old grandpa with creased, smiling eyes. He is the one who gave us every good gift. He is the source of all that is good—the small gifts and the grand ones.

He is watching it unfold—all of his kids taking pleasure in the cakes they've each been given and taking pleasure in the delight of each other.

And it brings him great joy, because this is all a gift, his *gift* to us. *Take and eat,* he is saying to us. *You have permission.*

It's like one big happiness cycle, set in motion by God.

Long ago, he made all of this for you. For you! He did not create this grand old world with hostile intentions. He did it with love.

Taste and see!

God delights in your delight.

He takes pleasure in your pleasure.

He built the "sweet" right into your sweet spot, not that you would turn from him, but that you might draw nearer to him.

Trust him with the gifts. Trust him with your happiness.

How appalling it would be if God did not take delight in our delight. How tragic it would be if God created us to seek happiness but then withheld from us our deepest desires. But that's not who God is. He gave us everything we need, and a million more things besides—things we never thought to ask for.

It's ours for the taking.

But it doesn't end with our pleasure alone. Oh no. You see, this is all for *his* pleasure. *This is all about God.* Our happiness brings him happiness. And that's why this is the holiest desire of all.

This is the law of the happiness cycle: The more you enjoy God, the happier you'll be. The happier you are, the more you'll pour out your happiness into the lives of others. The more you pour out your happiness into the lives of others, the happier they'll be. And the more we all experience and share that happiness, the more we bring delight to the Giver.

Imagine the smile of God, widening way up into his eyes as he whispers to all of heaven: "They really are something, aren't they?"

We've dared to taste happiness. We've learned how we're wired for it.

And now we're being asked to share it.

We, the dare takers, have become the dare sharers.

This is how our happiness changes the world.

Anyone with a heart beating inside of her has the capacity for happiness. But the ones who know Jesus should be happiest of all. Because no matter what happens in this life, we still have Jesus.

Someone can try to steal our happiness, but they can never steal our Jesus.

We are part of a happiness cycle that rotates forever on the axis of the Cross, a cycle that will carry us all the way home.

But until that day, well . . . here we are, wherever we are. There are a whole lot of people sharing this planet with us. Some of them are sad. Some are lonely. They have cakes, too, but they don't know what to do with them. They need someone to show them. They are asking the same questions we've been asking.

You, dear friend, have the answers.

You know that there is a happiness cycle and that it begins with God—who invented happiness and who has been shamelessly enticing us to chase after it. And just think: Those cakes we've been given are microscopic in comparison to the fantastic happiness that awaits us in heaven.

C. S. Lewis once noted that we humans can be awfully shy about mentioning heaven nowadays. "We are afraid of the jeer about 'pie in the sky,' and of being told that we are trying to 'escape' from the duty of making a happy world here and now into dreams of a happy world elsewhere." But, he added, without the hope of heaven, Christianity is false. As Christians, he said, we have a duty to think about heaven because the doctrine of heaven is woven into the whole fabric of what we believe. He said, "There have been times when I think we do not desire heaven; but more often I find myself wondering whether, in our heart of hearts, we have ever desired anything else."[2]

All that happiness you desire? In your heart of hearts, you are really longing for heaven.

Once upon a time, God came down from heaven to bring a piece of heaven for you. Like a bit of cake, a happy little taste of what's to come.

Thy happy Kingdom come, on earth as it is in heaven.

Look how he has set it before you. We're all sitting here with our little cakes. Isn't that something? God is seeing it all, like some wide-eyed grandpa just bursting with pride.

Listen for his voice, now, that whisper in your ear: *"Go on now, dig in, honey. It's all yours!"*

The Experiencer

The Relater

The Doer

What's Your Happiness Style? Assessment

The Giver

The Thinker

In just five minutes, the happiness style assessment will help you uncover your personal happiness style.

There are five styles of happiness—five ways that people are uniquely wired by God to experience delight in their daily lives. Your personal style reveals how you are primarily wired to experience happiness.

This test is not intended to quantify how happy you are. Rather, it is intended to single out your primary style so you can maximize your happiness in the way God made you.

There are no "right" answers or superior happiness styles. Just because you're strongest in one area doesn't mean you're weak in all the others. The results simply help you discover where you flourish when it comes to happiness.

As you read the possible answers to each numbered statement below, rate yourself according to how frequently or infrequently each response fits you, using the following scale.

1 = never
2 = rarely
3 = sometimes
4 = very often
5 = always

Try not to overthink your answers or score yourself based on how you *think* you should respond. Be honest with yourself in order to reach the truest result.

People who know me are likely to describe me as:

____   1. fun loving
____   2. contemplative

____ 3. generous

____ 4. purpose driven

____ 5. friendly

I am happiest when I'm:

____ 6. with other people

____ 7. learning or processing new ideas

____ 8. doing something for those who can't do it for themselves

____ 9. performing tasks that closely align with my purpose in the world

____ 10. lost in a moment, such as watching the sun rise or set

If I am on a trip, I am most likely to:

____ 11. be the one with the map and schedule

____ 12. enjoy reading the plaques underneath every exhibit at the museum

____ 13. enjoy time spent with those I love far more than any of the sights we might see

____ 14. be the one who planned it

____ 15. be the person treating everyone to a cappuccino or soda or leaving goodie bags in my co-travelers' hotel rooms to make them feel special and loved

I would be lost without:

____ 16. my to-do list

____ 17. a tribe of very close friends

____ 18. my books

____ 19. time set aside for adventure or vacations

____ 20. my ability to help other people

If I am at a social function, I am most likely to:

___ 21. enjoy getting to know the other people who are attending

___ 22. enjoy skipping the small talk and having a more in-depth conversation with one or two people

___ 23. enjoy finding a way to make the people around me feel cared for and encouraged

___ 24. enjoy organizing the fun activities that make the party especially memorable

___ 25. enjoy helping the host in the kitchen, rather than sitting down to chat with the other guests

If I had tomorrow afternoon free, I would most enjoy it by:

___ 26. reading a book or listening to a podcast

___ 27. being productive in tasks at home, at the office, or in the yard

___ 28. inviting a friend over

___ 29. taking part in a leisurely activity, such as taking a walk at a beautiful park, playing a round of golf, or going for a swim

___ 30. doing whatever my family or friends prefer to do

On the whole, I most enjoy life when I am:

___ 31. being useful

___ 32. in the company of friends

___ 33. learning and making new discoveries

___ 34. relaxing on the back deck under the stars

___ 35. making other people happy

If given a choice, I'd prefer:

___ 36. doing productive work more than taking a walk through the park

___ 37. spending Saturday night alone watching a documentary more than attending the block party down the street

___ 38. participating in a service project more than reading a book

___ 39. a day of spontaneous, unplanned adventure more than accomplishing purposeful work

___ 40. getting an invitation to a dinner party with friends more than free tickets to the hottest new play or musical act performing in my city

I typically feel energized:

___ 41. after a weeklong vacation

___ 42. after completing tasks

___ 43. when I attend social functions

___ 44. when I help someone

___ 45. when I have space and time to contemplate

People say I:

___ 46. am a daydreamer

___ 47. accomplish a lot in a day

___ 48. love a good time

___ 49. am easy to talk to

___ 50. am kindhearted toward family and friends

How to Score Your Test

Use the following tables to record your results. The top row in each table lists question numbers from the assessment, along with the happiness style to which they correspond. Transfer your answer to each numbered question to the appropriate square.

Add up your answers and write the total in the right-hand box. Your highest score is your primary happiness style. Your second-highest score is your secondary happiness style.

In the **DOERS** table, write down your scores for the following questions:

4	9	11	16	25	27	31	36	42	47	Doers Total:

In the **RELATERS** table, write down your scores for the following questions:

5	6	13	17	21	28	32	40	43	49	Relaters Total:

In the **EXPERIENCERS** table, write down your scores for the following questions:

1	10	14	19	24	29	34	39	41	48	Experiencers Total:

In the **GIVERS** table, write down your scores for the following questions:

3	8	15	20	23	30	35	38	44	50	Givers Total:

In the **THINKERS** table, write down your scores for the following questions:

2	7	12	18	22	26	33	37	45	46	Thinkers Total:

Read the descriptions on pages 65–66 to find out a bit more about your style. Then return to the chapters of *The Happiness Dare* to discover what your style means for you.

Most of us have a primary happiness style (your highest score) and a strong secondary happiness style (your second-highest score). Some people, however, score similarly across more than one happiness style.

No matter what your personal style is, I encourage you to read all five of the happiness-style chapters. We all have much to learn from the other types. Furthermore, each chapter will provide you with insights into your family and friends, who may have happiness styles that differ from your own.

Now that you know your results, here's where you flourish:

If you are a Doer . . .
You find supreme happiness in purposeful activity. You are in your sweet spot of happiness when you are doing what you were created to do—and doing it well. You are a list maker, an enthusiastic task juggler, and the kind of person who takes great

delight in fulfilling your purpose in the world. You are depend-able and goal oriented. You don't wait for the weekend to live the happy life God intended for you.

Find out more about Doers beginning on page 73.

If you are a Relater . . .

You find supreme happiness in positive, meaningful relation-ships with others. You are in your sweet spot of happiness when you are in the company of friends and family. You are an inviter, a lover, and a soul connector. You are known for being loving and warmhearted. You understand deeply that one of the great-est determinants of happiness is belonging.

Find out more about Relaters beginning on page 91.

If you are an Experiencer . . .

You find supreme happiness by engaging in meaningful moments with a sense of adventure, curiosity, and whimsy—at home or on the road. You are in your sweet spot of happiness when you engage the world with your deep sense of wonder. You are a beauty seeker, adventurer, and pay-attentioner. You are mindful and fun loving. You don't look for happiness in a store; you look for it in moments.

Find out more about Experiencers beginning on page 111.

If you are a Giver . . .

You find supreme happiness by seeking ways to bring delight to others. You are in your sweet spot when you find happiness by creating it for someone else. You are a helper, a sharer, and a light bearer. You are known for being thoughtful and selfless. You believe that a shared happiness is a double happiness.

Find out more about Givers beginning on page 133.

If you are a Thinker . . .
You find supreme happiness in the contemplative work of the mind. You take delight in learning, pondering, and dreaming. You are in your sweet spot when you push the limits of your beautiful, inquisitive mind. You are a noticer, a daydreamer, and a question asker. You are known for being curious and wise. You understand that the quality of your thinking is proportional to the depth of your happiness.

Find out more about Thinkers beginning on page 153.

Acknowledgments

~

I have developed this habit of reading acknowledgments first, before I start a book, because I want to know the heart of the author. And one of the best ways to know the heart of anyone is to meet the people who are a part of her life. These are my people—the ones who make me laugh, make me better, make me strong, and make me happy.

I offer my deepest thanks to these:

Mom and Dad—I dedicated this book to you because you *lived* with your whole selves what I was trying to say with written words. Thank you for showing me what durable happiness looks like, even when life threw you one curveball after another.

Scott—You are my favorite person in the world. You understand me like no one else ever has or ever will. You give me a hundred reasons every day to smile. Happiness is sharing this life with you.

Lydia and Anna—One of my greatest joys is having the privilege of being your mom. When you were little, I would sing to you, "You are my sunshine, my only sunshine. You make me happy when skies are gray." You still do.

Deidra, Shelly, and Michelle—I don't know what I'd do without our little Facebook group. Thanks for putting up with me on a regular basis. So often you've made me laugh when I thought I could only cry. You make me feel sane, despite my inner crazy!

Holley, Renee, and Kristen—You three have spoken so much wisdom into this book. Holley, your insights at key points in this journey were invaluable. Renee, it was you who first reminded me that miserable Christians make lousy public relations agents for Jesus—and then you loaned me the Swope family sunroom to write some of the most important paragraphs of this book. Kristen, your enthusiasm for this project has kept me moving forward.

Those mentioned in the book—including Carla, for your example as a happy Doer; Sandy, for teaching me to color outside the lines; Michelle, for being the happiest answer to my prayer for a friend; Sarah, for introducing me to "mandatory fun"; Jenn, for being an unstoppable Giver; Yettee, for sharing your beautiful, happy mind; Sally, for showing us all what it means to be a "There you are" person in a world that screams, "Here I am"; Anthony from Mayo Clinic, for bringing us a song when we didn't know how to sing.

Jennifer E.—Your battle to win back your joy has changed me for good. Thank you for offering me the rare privilege of sharing your story. Someday in heaven, I will hug your sweet Autumn and tell her what a beautiful mama she has.

My agent, Bill Jensen, as well as the entire team at Tyndale Momentum—Thanks for generously believing in me. Your wisdom has made all the difference.

My family and dear friends—Your unspoken names are

woven into the spine of this book and into the fabric of my life. I am indebted.

You, dear readers—You've shown up. You've prayed. You've shared my words with your friends. I love being in community with you! Now go get your happy on!

Jesus—"Come," you said to me, "and share your master's happiness." And so I did. I hopped on the back of the lion to ride these hills, and I will keep riding until I reach the gates of heaven. Until then, I pray: "Thy happy Kingdom come, on earth as it is in heaven."

Notes

𝒴

CHAPTER 1: STALKING HAPPINESS

1. Ecclesiastes 1:2
2. Matthew 6:34; Matthew 11:30
3. Blaise Pascal, *Pensées*, VII: "Morality and Doctrine."
4. John 16:33
5. Randy Alcorn, *Happiness* (Carol Stream, IL: Tyndale House, 2015), ix.
6. C. S. Lewis introduced the Christ figure Aslan, a lion, in the classic Chronicles of Narnia series.
7. Flannery O'Connor, *The Habit of Being: Letters of Flannery O'Connor* (New York: Farrar, Straus and Giroux, 1979), 126.
8. Anne Frank, *The Diary of a Young Girl* (New York: Bantam, 1993), 171.

CHAPTER 2: THE HOLY PURSUIT OF HAPPINESS

1. Matthew 25:21
2. Zephaniah 3:17
3. Matthew 19:14, NIV
4. For more on this topic, I recommend *Between Heaven and Mirth: Why Joy, Humor, and Laughter Are at the Heart of the Spiritual Life* by James Martin. (New York, NY: HarperOne, 2011). In the book, Martin opens the Gospels to reveal Jesus as a man of great joy and even playfulness. He argues that a humorless Jesus may be close to heretical.
5. See Matthew 5:1-12, GNT
6. Ibid.
7. John Piper, *Seeing and Savoring Jesus Christ* (Wheaton, IL: Crossway, 2004), 36.
8. Ibid., 35-36.
9. Matthew Henry, *Commentary on the Whole Bible*, vol. III (Christian Classics Ethereal Library).

10. Alcorn, *Happiness*, 52.
11. John 15:11. Two translations of the Bible use the word *happy* or *happiness* instead of *joy* in John 15:11. In the Contemporary English Version, for instance, John 15:11 reads: "I have told you this to make you as completely happy as I am."
12. Joni Eareckson Tada, *More Precious Than Silver: 366 Daily Devotional Readings* (Grand Rapids, MI: Zondervan, 1998), November 28 entry.
13. John Piper, "The Essential Warfare for Happiness," transcript of January 26, 2013, podcast, http://www.desiringgod.org /resource-library/ask-pastor-john/the-essential-warfare-for-holiness.
14. Matthew 6:10

CHAPTER 3: THE HAPPINESS DARE
1. Matthew 7:7
2. Westminster Shorter Catechism

CHAPTER 4: THE IMPORTANCE OF FINDING YOUR HAPPINESS STYLE
1. John 15:11, CEV
2. 1 Corinthians 12:18, MSG
3. 1 Corinthians 12:4, TLB
4. 1 Corinthians 12:4, MSG
5. To consider for yourself how likely it was that Bezalel, Oholiab, Tabitha, and Barnabas found happiness in their work, read Exodus 31:1-6, Acts 9:36-41, and Acts 4:36.
6. Colossians 1:27
7. John Calvin, "Man Now Deprived of Freedom of Will and Miserably Enslaved" in *Institutes of the Christian Religion*, trans. Henry Beveridge, Book Second (first published in 1845).
8. James 1:17, NASB
9. A. W. Tozer, *Who Put Jesus on the Cross? And Other Questions of the Christian Faith* (Camp Hill, PA: WingSpread Publishers, 1976).

CHAPTER 5: THE DOER
1. This part of Martha's story is told in Luke 10:38-42.
2. Elisabeth Elliot, *Discipline: The Glad Surrender* (Grand Rapids, MI: Revell, 1982), 126, emphasis added.
3. Colossians 3:23
4. Brother Lawrence and Frank Laubach, *Practicing His Presence* (Jacksonville, FL: SeedSowers, 1973), 103, 36.
5. John 11:5
6. crap stack (n): A gigantic tower of papers, bills, and lost spelling lists that build up over-time on account of laziness and/or denial. I don't know where the term *crap stack* originated, but I first learned of this perfect phrase from my friends Trish and Robbie.

7. Gretchen Rubin, "Make Your Bed," August 28, 2009, https://gretchenrubin .com/happiness_project/2009/08/make-your-bed/.

8. "Then Simon Peter arrived and went inside. He also noticed the linen wrappings lying there, while the cloth that had covered Jesus' head was folded up and lying apart from the other wrappings" (John 20:6-7, NLT).

CHAPTER 6: THE RELATER

1. Genesis 2:18

2. Ian Sample, "Loneliness Twice as Unhealthy as Obesity for Older People, Study Finds," *The Guardian*, February 16, 2014, https://www.theguardian .com/science/2014/feb/16/loneliness-twice-as-unhealthy-as-obesity -older-people.

3. Jon Clifton, "Mood of the World Upbeat on International Happiness Day," Gallup.com, March 19, 2015, http://www.gallup.com/poll/182009 /mood-world-upbeat-international-happiness-day.aspx.

4. Suzan Haskins and Dan Prescher, "Why Latin American Countries Are the Happiest," *Huffington Post*, June 12, 2015, http://www.huffingtonpost.com /suzan-haskins-and-dan-prescher/latin-american-countries-happiest_b _7012544.html.

5. Mark Vernon, a philosopher and psychotherapist, explores this in his book *The Meaning of Friendship* (Hampshire, England: Palgrave Macmillan, 2010).

6. John Donne, "Meditation XVII," *Devotions upon Emergent Occasions*.

7. Tori DeAngelis, "How Do Mind-Body Interactions Affect Breast Cancer?" *Monitor on Psychology* 33, no. 6 (June 2002), http://www.apa.org/monitor /jun02/mindbody.aspx.

8. See John 15:15 and Mark 9:2-3.

9. Matthew 17:1

10. Mark 14:34

11. John 15:12-14, NRSV

12. See Romans 12:15, NASB.

13. "What a Friend We Have in Jesus," lyrics by Joseph M. Scriven, written in 1855; public domain.

14. Sonja Lyubomirsky, *The How of Happiness: A New Approach to Getting the Life You Want* (New York: Penguin Press, 2008), 126.

CHAPTER 7: THE EXPERIENCER

1. Ann Voskamp, *One Thousand Gifts* (Grand Rapids, MI: Zondervan, 2010), 104.

2. Ibid.

3. Ibid., 105.

4. Saint Augustine, *The Works of Aurelius Augustine*, ed. Marcus Dobs (Edinburgh: T. & T. Clark, 1872), 13.

5. Jay Cassano, "The Science of Why You Should Spend Your Money on Experiences, Not Things," *Fast Company's Co.Exist*, March 30, 2015, http://www.fastcoexist.com/3043858/world-changing-ideas/the-science-of-why-you-should-spend-your-money-on-experiences-not-thing.
6. James Hamblin, "Buy Experiences, Not Things," *The Atlantic*, October 7, 2014, http://www.theatlantic.com/business/archive/2014/10/buy-experiences/381132/.
7. This story is told in, and quotes are taken from, John 21:1-19.
8. John 21:25
9. David Naugle, *Reordered Love, Reordered Lives* (Grand Rapids, MI: Eerdmans, 2008), 21.
10. C. S. Lewis, *The Weight of Glory and Other Addresses* (Grand Rapids, MI: Eerdmans, 1965), 1-2.
11. John Piper, *Desiring God* (Colorado Springs, CO: Multnomah Books, 2011), 20.
12. Robert Holden, "What Is Destination Addiction?" RobertHolden.org, http://www.robertholden.org/blog/what-is-destination-addiction/.
13. My pig farmer husband thanks you.

CHAPTER 8: THE GIVER
1. Isaiah 58:10, NASB, emphasis added.
2. Shawn Achor, "A Renewable Source of Joy: Giving Is the Foundation of Delight," *Success*, September 10, 2013, http://www.success.com/article/a-renewable-source-of-joy.
3. Shawn Achor, *Before Happiness: The 5 Hidden Keys to Achieving Success, Spreading Happiness, and Sustaining Positive Change* (New York: Crown Business, 2013).
4. Arthur Brooks, "Why Giving Makes You Happy," *New York Sun*, December 28, 2007, http://www.nysun.com/opinion/why-giving-makes-you-happy/68700/.
5. Acts 20:35, NLT
6. Psalm 118:24, NASB
7. Hebrews 12:2, NASB, emphasis added.

CHAPTER 9: THE THINKER
1. Proverbs 9:10
2. Richard S. Westfall, *The Life of Isaac Newton* (New York: Cambridge University Press, 1993), 16-17.
3. Mitch Stokes, *Christian Encounters: Isaac Newton* (Nashville: Thomas Nelson, 2010), 2.
4. Teun Koetsier, ed. and Luc Bergmans, ed., *Mathematics and the Divine: A Historical Study* (San Diego, CA: Elsevier Science, 2004), 461.
5. Psalm 8:3-4

6. Isaiah 1:18, KJV
7. Thank you to Seth Haines for first pointing this out to me.
8. *Merriam-Webster's Collegiate Dictionary*, 11th ed., s.v. *contemplate*.
9. 1 Corinthians 2:16
10. E. B. White, *Charlotte's Web* (New York: Harper & Row, 1952), 108-109.
11. Mihaly Csikszentmihalyi wrote about this in his classic book *Flow* (New York: Harper & Row, 1990). See also https://www.ted.com/speakers /mihaly_csikszentmihalyi.
12. Stokes, *Isaac Newton*, 22.
13. Romans 12:2, NLT
14. Thomas Brooks, "The Crown and Glory of Christianity," *The Complete Works of Thomas Brooks*, vol. 4.
15. See Isaiah 41:10, NLT; Matthew 28:20, KJV; John 14:27; Romans 8:38-39 (paraphrase).
16. See Titus 1:2.
17. Philippians 4:8

CHAPTER 10: FIVE MINUTES TO A HAPPIER YOU
1. This story—a modern-day parable—was told in 2000 on the TV drama *The West Wing*, season 2, episode 10, "Nöel."
2. Hebrews 2:18, MSG
3. Piper, *Desiring God*, 1st rev. ed. (Colorado Springs, CO: Multnomah, 2011), 28.
4. Philippians 4:8
5. Eun Kyung Kim, "New Study Finds Faith, Religion Can Help Provide 'Sustained Happiness,'" *Today*, November 6, 2015, http://www.today.com /kindness/study-religion-faith-can-help-provide-sustained-happiness-t39036.
6. Romans 5:3-4, NLT
7. Sally Quinn, "Religion Is a Sure Route to True Happiness," *Washington Post*, January 24, 2014, https://www.washingtonpost.com/national/religion /religion-is-a-sure-route-to-true-happiness/2014/01/23/f6522120-8452-11e3 -bbe5-6a2a3141e3a9_story.html.
8. "Native American Legends: Two Wolves," www.FirstPeople.us, http://www.firstpeople.us/FP-Html-Legends/TwoWolves-Cherokee.html.
9. 2 Corinthians 10:5
10. Caroline Leaf, *Switch On Your Brain: The Key to Peak Happiness, Thinking, and Health* (Grand Rapids, MI: Baker Books, 2013), 85.
11. Ibid., 38.
12. Romans 12:2
13. Maria Konnikova, "The Power of Concentration," *New York Times*, December 15, 2012, http://www.nytimes.com/2012/12/16/opinion/sunday/the-power -of-concentration.html?_r=1.

CHAPTER 11: THE PRINCIPLE OF SMALL DAILY GAINS

1. Proverbs 23:7, KJV
2. Jane Porter, "How to Rewire Your Brain for Greater Happiness," quoting Rick Hanson, author of *Hardwiring Happiness*, Fast Company, August 27, 2014, http://www.fastcompany.com/3034801/the-future-of-work/how-to-rewire -your-brain-for-greater-happiness.
3. William J. Cromie, "Meditation Found to Increase Brain Size," *Harvard Gazette*, February 2, 2006, http://news.harvard.edu/gazette/story/2006 |/02/meditation-found-to-increase-brain-size/.
4. Matthew 11:28, NLT
5. Caroline Leaf, *Switch On Your Brain* (Grand Rapids, MI: Baker Books, 2013), 22.
6. For more on the science behind the malleable brain, I recommend *Switch On Your Brain* by Caroline Leaf, *Hardwiring Happiness* by Rich Hanson, and *The How of Happiness* by Sonja Lyubomirsky.
7. Shawn Achor, *The Happiness Advantage: The Seven Principles of Positive Psychology That Fuel Success and Performance at Work* (New York: Crown Business, 2010), 97.
8. Lyubomirsky, *The How of Happiness: A Scientific Approach to Getting the Life You Want*, 20–22.
9. Ibid., 64.

CHAPTER 12: THE PRINCIPLE OF GOOD ENOUGH

1. Eric Barker, "How to Find Happiness in Today's Hectic World," *Barking Up the Wrong Tree* (blog), February 22, 2015, http://www.bakadesuyo.com/2015 /02/how-to-find-happiness/.
2. Colossians 3:23, MSG
3. Eric Barker, "Are Olympic Bronze Medalists Happier Than Silver Medalists?" *Barking Up the Wrong Tree* (blog), June 13, 2011, http://www.bakadesuyo.com /2011/06/are-olympic-bronze-medalists-happier-than-sil/.
4. Exodus 4:13, CEV
5. Judges 6:15, MSG
6. Matthew 5:12, GNT
7. Romans 12:15
8. Galatians 5:25-26, MSG

CHAPTER 13: THE PRINCIPLE OF PUTTING UP YOUR DUKES

1. Adam Weber is pastor of Embrace Church in Sioux Falls, South Dakota. You can watch his services online at www.iamembrace.com.
2. John 16:33, emphasis added
3. See John 11:35.
4. See Psalm 56:8, NLT
5. Nehemiah 8:10, emphasis added

6. Mark Siddall, "Serotonin: Pleasure or Pain?" IFLScience, August 19, 2014, http://www.iflscience.com/plants-and-animals/serotonin-pleasure-or-pain.
7. Nick Hytrek, "Orange City Day Care Provider Sentenced to 100 Years in 3-Year-Old's Death," *Sioux City Journal*, October 17, 2014.
8. Psalm 88:18
9. John 15:11, CEV
10. Hebrews 12:2, emphasis added

CHAPTER 14: THE PRINCIPLE OF THE HEAD-TO-FOOT ALLELUIA
1. Psalm 78:25
2. Numbers 11:4
3. Numbers 14:2
4. Corrie ten Boom, *The Hiding Place* (Washington Depot, CT: Chosen Books, 1971), 180.
5. Ibid., 183.
6. Ibid., 192.
7. Luke 17:15-19, ESV
8. "In Praise of Gratitude," Harvard Health Publications, November 1, 2011, http://www.health.harvard.edu/newsletter_article/in-praise-of-gratitude.
9. Shawn Achor, *The Happiness Advantage* (New York: Crown Business, 2010), 100.
10. Voskamp, *One Thousand Gifts*, 58.

CHAPTER 15: THE HAPPINESS CYCLE
1. One study says it is totally normal to want to squeeze cute children and adorable puppies. Liz Langley, "When We See Something Cute, Why Do We Want to Squeeze It?" *National Geographic*, October 10, 2015, http://news.nationalgeographic.com/2015/10/151010-science-psychology-babies-animals-culture-behavior/.
2. C. S. Lewis, *The Problem of Pain*, rev. ed. (New York, HarperCollins, revised edition 2009), 149.

About the Author

Jennifer Dukes Lee, author of *Love Idol* and *The Happiness Dare*, is a storyteller and a grace dweller. She is a popular blogger, an (in)courage writer, and a frequent speaker who can't get over God's amazing grace. Her writing has appeared at Women of Faith, *Today's Christian Woman*, *Relevant*, the blogs of Ann Voskamp and Holley Gerth, TheBetterMom.com, and many others.

Jennifer is a former award-winning news reporter who covered crime, politics, and natural disasters for several Midwestern metropolitan daily newspapers. Now she uses her reporting skills to chase after the biggest story ever: the redemptive story of Christ.

She clings to the hope of the Cross and is passionate about sharing the Good News through story. She believes in miracles; she is one. She marvels at God's unrelenting grace for people who mess up—stumbling sinners like her, who have been made whole through Christ.

Jennifer and her husband live on the Lee family farm in Iowa with their two daughters, where they spend at least five minutes every day in the pursuit of happiness. Jennifer attends a small country church, and some Sundays you can find her in the back of the sanctuary, spinning tunes as the church deejay. She loves air guitar, dark chocolate, emojis, messy people, and Jesus—not in that order. Visit Jennifer online at www.JenniferDukesLee.com.

She invites you to join her on Twitter and Instagram @dukeslee and on Facebook at /JenniferDukesLee.

Hey, Dare Taker!

What a ride, eh? The good news is, it's not over!
This Happiness Dare is just beginning for you.

There's a whole community of us Dare Takers out here,
and we want to celebrate happiness with you.

Join us by using #TheHappinessDare
on Instagram, Facebook, and Twitter.
Together, we are pursuing our heart's deepest,
holiest, and most vulnerable desire.

VISIT WWW.THEHAPPINESSDARE.COM

to discover your happiness style and find other
resources to cultivate happiness in your life.

CONNECT WITH JENNIFER

JENNIFERDUKESLEE.COM

@DUKESLEE

FOR MORE OF JENNIFER'S JOURNEY,
DON'T MISS HER BOOK *LOVE IDOL:
LETTING GO OF YOUR NEED FOR APPROVAL—
AND SEEING YOURSELF THROUGH GOD'S EYES*

CP1137